Selected Studies of
Classroom Teaching:
A Comparative Analysis

Selected Studies of Classroom Teaching: A Comparative Analysis

SELMA BETTY GREENBERG
Hofstra University

INTERNATIONAL TEXTBOOK COMPANY
An Intext *Publisher*
Scranton, Pennsylvania 18515

371.3
H798a

72-4595

ISBN 0-7002-2285-5

To Bill, Lisa, Andrew, and Ellen

Contents

Tables

Figures

Selected Studies of
Classroom Teaching:
A Comparative Analysis

I

Background of the Study

Since the mid 1950s, new areas of study have been identified for the researcher and theorist in the area of curriculum and teaching. Believing that the ultimate goal of classroom prediction and control will be reached only after a long process of research and theory definition and redefinition, a number of classroom researchers have embarked on large-scale observational studies of classroom teaching and behavior. It is the hope that these studies will provide the data both for more firmly grounded theoretical concepts of curriculum and teaching, and for future studies of an experimental nature. These efforts at descriptive research were stimulated through the work of Marie M. Hughes and B. O. Smith:

> This expressed need to know more intimately the life of children in the classroom prompted us to work as we have. We believe that more information was needed to know what actually happened in the classroom day after day. With this information teaching could be described in a more useful manner. We asked the questions: What do teachers actually do? What is school life like for children?[1]
>
> Since descriptive research is sometimes depreciated, perhaps something should be said in its defense. If very little is known about a phenomenon, the way to begin an investigation of it is to observe and analyze the phenomenon itself. It must be observed, analyzed, and classified into its various elements. Until the factors which are involved in the phenomena are understood and described, there is little likelihood that significant correlational, predictive, or causal studies can be made.[2]

The studies in the same genre as Smith and Hughes' are designed partially or wholly to reveal how indeed teaching and "pupil-ing" and classroom interaction proceeds in some sample of the American school system. The studies of Bellack, Flanders, and Taba, like those of Hughes and Smith, are all examples or partial examples of the descriptive mode of investigation. However, each researcher has de-

---

[1] Marie M. Hughes and Associates, "The Assessment of the Quality of Teaching: A Research Report," U.S. Office of Education, Cooperative Research Project No. 353 (Salt Lake City: University of Utah, 1959), p. 8.

[2] B. Othanel Smith and Milton O. Meux, "A Study of the Logic of Teaching" (Urbana: University of Illinois, College of Education, Bureau of Educational Research, 1963), p. 8.

veloped his own unique set of definitions, style of description, and pattern of analysis. In the spring of 1965 Phillip Jackson delivered an address[3] in which he briefly assessed the field of research in teaching, indicated areas in which adequate descriptions had been begun and other areas in which further descriptive research was needed, and suggested that an intensive and extensive analysis of the work already completed could be of value.

The purpose of this work is to analyze and render explicit those areas of convergence and divergence in the studies of Bellack, Flanders, Hughes, Smith, and Taba. Thus will be demonstrated where new research is needed, where already completed research needs explication and extension, and where the beginnings of a general classificatory system for classroom behavior may be rooted.

Although originally a two-volume report, the Bellack study is now published in a single volume. The Smith work is reported in two volumes which, however, here will be treated as one.

To discuss any of these studies as if each were the work of one individual is to adopt a convention. Each of the five studies represents the work of a group of people, and that fact is acknowledged here. However, within the context of the present study, the convention of referring to each study by the name of the chief investigator seems justified.

THE TITLES

Arno Bellack, Herbert Kliebard, Ronald Hyman, and Frank Smith, *The Language of the Classroom* (New York: Teachers College Press, 1966).

Ned A. Flanders, "Teacher Influence, Pupil Attitudes, and Achievement," U.S. Office of Education, Cooperative Research Project No. 397 (Minneapolis: University of Minnesota, 1960).

Marie M. Hughes and Associates, "The Assessment of the Quality of Teaching: A Research Report," U.S. Office of Education, Cooperative Research Project No. 353 (Salt Lake City: University of Utah, 1959).

B. Othanel Smith and Milton O. Meux, in collaboration with others, "A Study of the Logic of Teaching" (Urbana: Bureau of Educational Research, College of Education, University of Illinois, 1963).

B. Othanel Smith and Milton O. Meux, "A Tentative Report on Strategies of Teaching," U.S. Office of Education, Department of Health, Education, and Welfare, Project No. 1640 (Urbana: Bureau

---

[3] Phillip Jackson, "The Way Teaching Is," *National Education Association Journal*, 54:10, November, 1965.

of Educational Research, College of Education, University of Illinois, 1964).

Hilda Taba and others, "Thinking in Elementary School Children," U.S. Department of Health, Education, and Welfare, Cooperative Research Program, Project No. 1574 (San Francisco: San Francisco State College, 1964).

QUESTIONS IN THE STUDY

This study was originally designed with two central foci: one, an examination of the specific issues arising from an investigation and analysis of each of the five studies, and the other, an examination of the issues which, though arising from these studies, were of more general interest to the curriculum and teaching researcher or theorist. To define and delineate these two major foci, both specific and more general questions were outlined.

SPECIFIC QUESTIONS

1. (a) What areas of curriculum and teaching have been sampled by these studies? (b) What area and aspects remain to be described?
2. (a) What are the assumptions that one can identify in each of these studies? (b) What agreement and what variation in basic assumptions exist between and among these studies?
3. (a) What is the design and scope of each study? (b) What are the differences and similarities in scope and design?
4. (a) What styles and systems of observation were used in each study? (b) How do these styles of observation vary from study to study?
5. (a) What categories of analysis and statistical systems were used in each study? (b) How do these styles of observation vary from study to study?
6. Can one categorize the studies in terms of specific characteristics?
7. (a) How effective has each study been in answering the questions posed at each study's inception? (b) Is there a relationship between effectiveness and research design, style and system of observation, and patterns of analysis?
8. Are there sufficient similarities in observational and analytical categories between or among these studies to suggest the beginnings of a general system for observation and analysis in the field of curriculum and teaching?

GENERAL QUESTIONS

1. What is the relation of research to theory in curriculum and teaching?

2. What is the relation of individuality of definition to communicability? If basic terms remain individually defined, what is the effect on intrafield and interfield communication?
3. What is the relation of evaluation to research? If evaluative terms are used in research, what is the effect on the dissemination and usefulness of the research?
4. What different kinds of relationships are possible between researcher and clinician and researcher and administrator and supervisor? Do these relationships vary with respect to the goals of the researcher?

PLAN OF THE STUDY

Originally it was thought that a discussion of the specific questions, stimulated by examination of the five studies, should precede discussion of questions of a more general nature. It was believed that this plan would enable the discussion of the specific questions to lead to a more adequate analysis of questions of more general interest. However, as work on the study proceeded, it became quite clear that specific issues raised by these studies were being analyzed in terms of a larger framework that includes a particular point of view. Paradoxically, this larger framework was evolving in response to insights gained from analysis and investigation into the specific issues. Thus, to mirror more closely the actual development of the study, and to offer the reader as detailed a picture as possible of the larger framework in which the specific issues raised by these five studies were analyzed, the original outline has been altered. Thus, discussion of the more general questions will precede, rather than follow, the examination of the specific questions.

Two further considerations arising from the actual analysis of the studies influenced the decision to alter the arrangement of the study. In planning this study, the great importance of those explicit and implicit assumptions present in research and theory seemed obvious. As the work progressed, this original impression was strengthened. All research studies make assumptions, and the studies herein being analyzed as well as the study being presented, are no exceptions. The diligent researcher and theorist endeavors to render his assumptions explicit, so that those who read and study his work may do so with sharpened insight. However, the very nature of the common-sense meaning of assumption (that is, act of taking for granted; suppositions; also the thing assumed) causes assumptions to be difficult to explicate. Thus, by detailing as much of the framework of analysis as possible, two results are intended. The reader may be better able to pursue his own analysis, both of the assumptions of the studies herein described and those of the study herein presented.

The second reason for discussing the general questions first arises from the major theme of this analysis, which is that of the concept of multiple interpretations. Not believing that the raw data of observation "speak for themselves," alternative opinions, judgments, and conclusions based on the same evidence will be suggested, noted, and documented, whenever appropriate, throughout this work. Therefore, the ease with which the lines of reasoning and argument can be followed throughout this study is crucial to the communicability of the study and its evaluation. These lines of reasoning will be most readily followed by using the revised plan of explicating the general questions first.

II

An Outline of the Studies Analyzed

THE LANGUAGE OF THE CLASSROOM

The Bellack study, "The Language of the Classroom," undertaken at Teachers College, Columbia University, New York, had as its purpose the investigation of the teaching process through an analysis of the teachers' and students' linguistic behavior. While the major goal of the study was the description of the teachers' and students' linguistic behavior, a secondary goal was the study of the relationship of linguistic variables to student learning and attitude change.

The subjects, drawn from the suburban and metropolitan New York area, were fifteen high school classes in a Problems of Democracy course: 345 students, fifteen teachers. An attempt was made to hold the content constant by having each teacher use the first four chapters of the pamphlet *International Economic Problems* by James Calderwood as the basis for their teaching. However, teachers were urged to teach the material in any manner they thought suitable. Four class sessions were recorded on tape for each of the fifteen classes.

The unit identified for analysis was termed "the pedagogical move." Four moves were identified: structuring, soliciting, responding, and reacting. It was found that moves serve different functions; thus structuring and soliciting moves were both seen as initiating moves, while responding and reacting moves were called reflexive moves. As analysis continued, it was apparent that moves occurred in patterns, called teaching cycles. A cycle contained some combination of moves.

Four functionally different types of meanings were abstracted from student-teacher communication: (1) *substantive* meanings with associated (2) *substantive* logical meanings; and (3) instructional meanings with associated (4) *instructional-logical* meanings.

After class sessions were recorded, all the discourse was typed into protocols in a standard fashion. When the lines were counted, the teacher-pupil ratio of spoken discourse was three to one. When pedagogical moves were counted, the ratio of teacher moves to pupil moves was three to two.

The pedagogical roles of teacher and pupil seem clearly defined. The teacher generally makes the initiatory moves and the students the reflexive moves. The teacher also reacts to the responses of the students. The studies reveal that the linguistic behavior of classes and teachers is remarkably similar among the fifteen teachers and classes and between class sessions. In general, structuring moves account for about 12 to 14 per cent of the discourse in terms of lines spoken, while the soliciting, responding, and reacting moves each account for about 20 to 40 per cent of the lines.

Bellack suggests that conceptualizing the results in terms of a classroom language game may be helpful for although classes differ somewhat, his results indicate that teachers and pupils play complementary roles in a game in which they appear to follow implicit rules.

TEACHER INFLUENCE, PUPIL ATTITUDES, AND ACHIEVEMENT

The Flanders study, "Teacher Influence, Pupil Attitudes, and Achievement," undertaken at the University of Minnesota, had as its primary concern investigation of spontaneous interaction between teacher and student. The central concept of the study was that of "classroom climate," defined as: ". . . generalized attitudes toward the teacher and the class that the pupils share in common despite individual differences."[1]

It was assumed, for the purposes of this study, that an analysis of the teacher's verbal behavior would warrant inferences about his expansion of or contraction of student freedom of action. As defined in the Flanders study, a teacher who sets restraints upon students or focuses student attention upon an idea is said to be exerting *direct influence*, while one who reduces restraints upon students and encourages student participation is said to be exerting *indirect influence*.

Before the major study was begun, preliminary studies of teacher influence and student attitudes were conducted in both Minnesota and New Zealand in the years 1955 to 1957. The subjects of the major study consisted of thirty-two classes in mathematics and social

---

[1] Ned A. Flanders, "Teacher Influence, Pupil Attitudes, and Achievement: Studies in Interaction Analysis," U.S. Office of Education, Cooperative Research Project No. 397 (Minneapolis: University of Minnesota, 1960), p. 3.

studies drawn from the Twin Cities School System. All students were on the junior high school level, the social studies classes selected from the seventh grade level, the mathematics classes from the eighth grade level.

Flanders reports that four distinct research tools were used in the investigation:

> ... First, an observation procedure called classroom interaction analysis; second, several student attitude inventories assessing student perceptions of the teacher and the schoolwork; third, a dependence-proneness test used for scaling this attribute among students; and fourth, achievement tests used to measure learning achievement.[2]

The results indicated that students in the classes identified as indirect, based on a rank order of the i/d (indirect to direct) ratio, achieved more than students in classes identified as direct. Additional evidence indicated that when student attitudes were favorable, higher achievement occurred. The indirect teachers, in both mathematics and social studies, managed their classes so as to permit students to express their opinions and participate more than did the teachers identified as direct. However, in mathematics, those teachers identified as indirect used both expanding and restricting types of activities more often than did the teachers identified as direct.

DEVELOPMENT OF MEANS FOR ASSESSMENT OF THE QUALITY OF TEACHING

Marie M. Hughes' study, "Development of the Means for the Assessment of the Quality of Teaching," was undertaken at the University of Utah. Originally this research was to deal with the problem of teacher rating. Having no wish to repeat the large number of unsuccessful studies based on teacher characteristics, traits, and training, and their relationship to teachers' effectiveness, Hughes decided to study teacher-pupil interaction in the classroom. The decision was made to begin with classroom description before attempting teacher evaluation.

Forty-one elementary school teachers, comprising three subgroups, were the subjects of the study. There were twenty-five judged-good teachers and ten representative teachers from one school. In calculating the results of the major study, the analysis included the records of six judged-good teachers from the pilot study that preceded the major investigation. Thus information was derived from the records of forty-one teachers.

[2] *Ibid.*, p. 18.

The basic data of this study are called specimen records. The data were secured through stenographic recordings by two classroom observers. The two observers collated their observational records and retained only that information upon which they could both agree. The records were taken for three thirty-minute periods for each teacher, except for the six teachers who comprised the pilot study, for whom there were four specimen records each.

The specimen records were analyzed using a code called "The University of Utah Revision of the Provo Code for the Analysis of Teaching." The twin concepts used in the development of this code were teacher power and teacher responsiveness. Within this twin concept structure, thirty-one teaching functions were identified and then grouped under seven categories: controlling, imposition, facilitating, content development, response, positive affectivity, and negative affectivity.

The results of the study indicated that the teachers' most pervasive and frequent function was in the category of control. In over two-thirds of the hundred and twenty-nine records, more than 40 per cent of all teaching acts fell into the category defined as control. Teachers also used functions of negative affectivity to control their groups. Teachers rarely expanded student ideas or acted as resource persons for students. Few functions of personal response were coded, although teachers were generally more positive than negative with the children.

THE LOGIC OF TEACHING AND A TENTATIVE REPORT OF THE STRATEGIES OF TEACHING

The two Smith studies, undertaken by the Bureau of Educational Research at the University of Illinois, are called "The Logic of Teaching" and "A Tentative Report of the Strategies of Teaching." Teaching, as defined by Smith, is essentially a system of social action, involving an end-in-view, an agent, and a situation. Smith dichotomizes the teaching situation into one set of elements, such as class size and characteristics of pupils, and one set of elements such as assignments and the asking of questions. Smith is concerned with the second set of characteristics, those characteristics that he describes as the means by which the ends-in-view are reached. Smith further discusses the teaching situation:

> The means, in turn, consists in two types of factors: subject matter and paraphernalia, and the ways of manipulating and maneuvering the subject matter and paraphernalia. The first of these we call material means and the second procedural means. The procedural means have

two aspects: large-scale movements which we call strategies, and smaller movements, constituting tactical elements of strategies, which we call logical operations.[3]

In Smith's first study, "The Logic of Teaching," classroom discourse was analyzed to discover the logical operations involved in teaching. Smith identified two classroom verbal patterns: the episode, a verbal exchange between two or more speakers, and the monologue, a solo performance by one speaker. The episodes were classified in terms of the episode's *entry* or opening statement or question.

In Smith's second study, he was concerned with the larger teaching maneuvers having to do with the control of the subject matter of instruction, the strategies. Strategies are concerned with attaining certain outcomes and are hence directly related to objectives. The data for analysis were obtained by taping the classroom discourse of seventeen high school classes from grades nine through twelve. The classes included three in English, three in mathematics, five in science, and six in history or social studies.

During the course of the first study, criteria for identifying and classifying the episode in terms of its entry were developed. This classification was in terms of the logical operations implied in the entry. An attempt was made to identify those logical operations which distinguish one subject from another.

During the course of the second study, the major focus was on the identification and classification of a unit designated as a *venture*. The venture was defined as: ". . . a segment of discourse consisting of a set of utterances dealing with a single topic and having a single overarching content objective."[4] Criteria for identifying nine such ventures were developed.

THINKING IN ELEMENTARY SCHOOL CHILDREN

Hilda Taba's study, "Thinking in Elementary School Children," was undertaken at the San Francisco State College. The study, which lasted for eighteen months, was regarded as exploratory in nature.

The subjects of the study consisted of twenty elementary school classes. Three classes at the second grade level, five at the third grade

[3] B. Othanel Smith and Milton O. Meux, "A Study of the Logic of Teaching" (Urbana: Bureau of Educational Research, College of Education, University of Illinois, 1963), p. 3.

[4] B. Othanel Smith and Milton O. Meux, "A Tentative Report on Strategies of Teaching," U.S. Office of Education, Department of Health, Education, and Welfare, Project No. 1640 (Urbana: Bureau of Educational Research, College of Education, University of Illinois, 1964), p. 5.

level, three at the fourth grade level, five at the fifth grade level, and four at the sixth grade level were selected.

The study has as its central objective the examination of the development of thought under optimum training conditions. Three criteria defined these optimal conditions: (1) a curriculum designed specifically toward the end of developing thinking, (2) teaching strategies that would focus explicitly and consciously on necessary cognitive skill mastery, and (3) sufficient time to allow for a developmental sequence in training.

To fulfill the first criterion, a curriculum designed for the development of thought was devised. The twenty classes involved in the study followed a social studies curriculum organized around basic ideas as targets for learning. In addition, the specially designed curriculum contained a detailed sequence of learning experiences.

To fulfill the second requirement of adequate teaching strategies, the twenty teachers received special training. Ten days were provided for training teachers; five of these days were used consecutively in August, and the remaining five days were spent in half-day training sessions throughout the school year. Two major areas covered in the training were:

I. The analysis of the structure and the rationale of the curriculum.

II. The training in the teaching strategies for the development of the skills involved in the three cognitive tasks.[5]

In addition to the already stated central objectives of the study, other subsidiary objectives were pursued. One such subsidiary objective was the development of a method of categorizing thought process. To fulfill this objective, a code was developed and used to analyze four discussions taped at different times of the year for each class. Another subsidiary objective was to examine the effect on the development of cognitive processes. To further this objective, both analysis of the classroom interaction was undertaken and a Social Studies Inference Test was developed and used.

[5] Hilda Taba and others, "Thinking in Elementary School Children," U.S. Department of Health, Education, and Welfare, Cooperative Research Program, Project No. 1574 (San Francisco: San Francisco State College, 1964), p. 58.

III

The Relation of Research to Theory in Curriculum and Teaching

The relation of research to theory can never be examined completely. However, if the subject is analyzed in terms of the different subtopics and subissues it raises, one may arrive at a more adequate discussion than if one were to attempt a unidimensional analysis.

The term "theory" is commonly defined in several different ways. Since each definition carries with it different implications and assumptions for theory building and theory development, it may be appropriate to begin our discussion of the larger issue with an investigation of this crucial term "theory." A theory, suggests one definition, is a set of logically interrelated propositions from which, by deduction, relationships can be demonstrated and new information derived. The significance of theory, by this definition, is that it can both explain phenomena and indicate the consequences of actions. Now, theory, thus defined, has had a happy and distinguished history in music, mathematics, and the physical sciences. Theory, in this sense, exists in none of the social sciences. It certainly does not exist in the field of curriculum and teaching at present. Whether or not the material with which the teaching researcher and theorist must work is capable of eventually yielding a firm theoretical base is a question that can be dealt with more adequately later.

When no firmly rooted theoretical framework exists, scientific inquiry may proceed in one of two alternative ways. Just as one deduces hypotheses to be tested from a firmly rooted theoretical framework, a large-scale theoretical framework may be hypothesized from which, by deduction, one can define testable hypotheses. Freudian theory in psychiatry is an example of this hypothetical-deductive approach to theory building. The alternative approach to theory building when no firm theoretical framework exists is an inductive approach—inductive in the sense that small-scale theories as hypotheses are empirically tested and, where validated, are combined and recombined to form larger, more abstract theories. Thus, the more abstract theories develop from numbers of less abstract ones. The following quotation by Baldwin, in which he speaks of theory building for the theorists who work in behavioral psychology, makes this distinction quite clear:

> The philosophy of scientific strategy held by general behavior theorists is to get along with the absolute minimum of concepts. They generally restrict their activities to a limited area and do not try to build a theory which is intended to encompass all behavior. Instead, they try to predict the behavior they have studied and by this process gradually enlarge the scope of the theory. Other theorists prefer a large vague theory which is all encompassing and proceed to refine it to fit the details of specific experiments. These are two ways that science can progress. Each has its assets and each has its liabilities. The broad theory may never become specific; the narrow theory may concentrate more and more effort on a better explanation of insignificant behavior. Probably the choice between the two depends more upon the personality of the scientist than upon the requirements of the subject matter.[1]

Much of the writings of educational theorists, philosophers, and others, which formerly were termed "theory" are now frequently called "prescriptive theory." Theory in this sense is a set of proposals for actions that are derived from more general statements concerning the nature of man, culture, society, thinking, and learning. The more general statements are often themselves based on faith, assumption, conjecture, and incomplete evidence, and so, generally, is the theory that derives from them. This general statement from which the set of proposals for action is derived may be identified as a philosophic or cognitive framework. Thus, Stratemeyer and others, in writing *Developing a Curriculum for Modern Living*, published in 1947, proposed that the educated man is one who has learned to deal effectively with his "persistent life situations." Beginning with this novel definition of the "educated man," Stratemeyer enunciated a detailed curriculum plan. This curriculum plan, when implemented, was to produce the "solver of persistent life situations." In 1957 Smith, Stanley, and Shores, in *Fundamentals of Curriculum Development*, declared that democracy is the central value of this country. Having announced what they believed the central value of the country to be, they wove a theory of curriculum which would, they claimed, develop the "democratic person." This "democratic person" was needed if the country's central value of democracy was to be maintained or attained. Most recently, in 1964, Phenix, in *Realms of Meaning*, stated

[1] Alfred Baldwin, *Behavior and Development in Childhood* (New York: Dryden Press, 1955), p. 583.

that man's distinguishing characteristic is his search for meaning. Following this statement of belief, Phenix, as had Stratemeyer and Smith earlier, suggests the guidelines for a curriculum. The adoption of the curriculum as proposed by Phenix would enable students to "engender meanings."

In the field of curriculum and teaching, the most commonly used meaning of theory has been in its prescriptive sense. Indeed, prescriptive theory's link with education is almost as old as philosophy. For are not Plato's and Aristotle's recommendations for schooling excellent examples of prescriptive theory? One might consider prescriptive theory as closely related to the hypothetical-deductive theories discussed earlier. However, in the past the prescriptive theories of educational theorists, philosophers, and others have not provided the researcher with a base from which testable hypotheses could be deduced, nor have they suggested the necessity for doing so. This may be the reason why the inductive approach to theory building is being urged as proper to the present state of the curriculum and theory field. This small-scale theory as hypothesis is here also being suggested as most probably productive for the teaching theorist at present.

Although suggesting that theory as hypothesis might be the most helpful definition of theory to adopt, it is not to be assumed that the researcher must view the relationship between theory and research as unidirectional. Theory is not only tested in research, but novel theoretical insights are gained within the research setting itself. Indeed, it might be suggested that in assigning primacy in time to theory rather than research, we are but assuming a convention. Dewey suggested that thought follows upon the perceptions of the data of reality and that formulation of explanatory concepts and theories follows observations: "Scientific method includes, in short, all the processes by which the observing and amassing of the data be regulated with a view to facilitating the formation of explanatory conceptions and theories."[2]

Whether one takes the view that theory is antecedent to research, or research is antecedent to theory, their interrelatedness is clear:

> All foresight, prediction, planning as well as theorizing and speculation, are characterized by excursion from the actual into the possible. Hence (as we have already seen) what is inferred demands a double test: first, the process of forming the idea or supposed solution is checked by constant cross reference to the conditions observed to be actually present; secondly, the idea after it is formed is tested by acting upon it

---

[2] John Dewey, *How We Think*, rev. ed. (Boston: D. C. Heath and Co., 1933), p. 20.

overtly if possible, otherwise in imagination. The consequences of this action confirm, modify, or refute the idea.[3]

Before continuing to examine the further ramifications of the relation of theory to research, it is important to consider an issue raised by the five studies here analyzed. Is research possible without theory? The position taken by Selltiz, Jahoda, Deutsch, and Cook on this issue is considered in this study to be justified:

> Whether or not the nature of the anticipated relationships can be stated explicitly—i.e., whether or not they can be expressed as hypotheses in the formulation stage of an inquiry—depends largely on the state of knowledge in the area under investigation. Scientific research can begin with well formulated hypotheses, or it can formulate hypotheses as the end product of the research.
>
> It goes without saying that the formulation and verification of hypotheses is a goal of scientific inquiry. Yet there is no short cut to this goal. In many areas of social relations, significiant hypotheses do not exist. Much exploratory research, therefore, must be done before hypotheses can be formulated. Such exploratory work is an inevitable step in scientific progress.[4]

To see the area of interest to the teaching researcher and theorist as pre-theoretical serves to heighten an understanding of the importance of the five studies here being analyzed. The need for research into the nature of teaching precedes the need for research based on hypotheses testing. This need has already been suggested as the need to know what indeed transpires in the classroom. Or as Mary Jane Aschner wrote: ". . . to find out how teachers actually do their job and what the job in actual practice turns out to be."[5]

When the object of research is to observe and describe, some kind of system for observation and description is necessary. Medley and Mitzel identify two alternative systems for descriptive research: the category system and the sign system:

> Two approaches to the construction of items for an observational schedule can be readily distinguished. The first approach is to limit the observation to one segment or aspect of classroom behavior, and construct a finite set of categories into one and only one of which every unit observed can be classified. The report obtained purports to show, for each period of observation, the total number of units of behavior which occurred and the number classifiable in each category. An approach of this type will be referred to as a category system.

[3]*Ibid.*, p. 14.

[4]Claire Selltiz, Marie Jahoda, Morton Deutsch, and Stuart W. Cook, *Research Methods in Social Relations* (New York: Holt, Rinehart, and Winston, 1963), p. 39.

[5]Mary Jane Aschner, "The Language of Teaching," *Teachers College Record*, 61:242, February, 1960.

The second approach is to list beforehand a number of specific acts or incidents of behavior which may not occur during a period of observation. The record will show which of these incidents occurred during the period of observation and, in some cases, how frequently each occurred. An approach of this type will be referred to as a sign system.[6]

All of the studies here being analyzed are of the first type, in that each one uses a category system. However, each study uses a category system for observation and description that is unique. Thus, when one generally accepted category system does not exist, descriptive studies can be placed somewhere on a continuum in respect to the origination of their category system. At one end of the continuum are those studies in which attempts are made to build categories for future description from both an empirical and a logical response to the raw data of observation. At the other end of the continuum are those studies that utilize a system of categories that the researcher himself or some other researcher or theoretician has already developed. In the first instance, that in which categories are to be built, of course some notion must exist as to how facts may be categorized or ordered, or no work could go forward. However, the extent to which the categories must fit the theory, or, conversely, the extent to which the "notions" are modified by the categories, is the crucial difference in determining in what way the category system was designed. An established category system may have developed from past research or from an a priori hypothesis that certain categories will yield a viable framework for description. In some already completed studies in this initial descriptive stage, classification follows or is carried on concurrently with description, while in other studies, description follows a theoretically or empirically established set of categories.

The Bellack and Smith studies can be placed at one end of the continuum, both Bellack and Smith having established their categories as they collected and examined their data. A description of the Bellack system for analysis is briefly discussed:

> Development of the code for analysis was a long and detailed process requiring the interaction of several researchers who constantly reviewed and revised successive approximations of the final code in the light of actual protocols. This provided an immediate empirical check for the more abstract concepts of analysis that gradually emerged in the course of the work. This daily encounter between meaning and the

[6] Donald Medley and Harold E. Mitzel, "Measuring Classroom Behavior by Systematic Observation," in N. L. Gage, ed., American Educational Research Association *Handbook of Research on Teaching* (Chicago: Rand McNally, 1963), p. 298.

empirical data of the classroom discussions provided a fruitful and realistic means for developing the system for analysis.[7]

Smith describes the establishment of his category system:

> Once recordings were made, transcribed, and reproduced in dittoed form, the task was to work out some suitable way of describing the discourse. One way to describe units of discourse is to analyze it into units. Of course, there are many different units of discourse—words, sentences, paragraphs, etc. But the purpose of this investigation made it necessary that the unit be related significantly to instruction. One of the units finally worked out is a unit of discourse beginning with an expression which triggers a verbal exchange about a topic and ending with a completion of the discussion of that topic. This unit we call an episode. The other unit of discourse, in which there is one and only one speaker, we refer to as a monolog.[8]

Of all five studies, Flanders' is the best example of a category system based on an already established system, and thus on the other end of the continuum from the Bellack and Smith studies. Flanders drew on the previous empirical and theoretical concepts of earlier researchers; the work of Anderson, Lippit, and White; Whithall, Perkins, and Cogan; and Flanders' own previous work enabled his study to begin with categories already established.

In Flanders' research on classroom climate, he pursued an investigation into social climate that has already established empirical and theoretical roots:

> ... When a teacher accepts, clarifies, or makes constructive use of a student's ideas or feelings, when he praises or encourages student behavior, and when he asks questions, he will usually be increasing the freedom of action of the students. On the other hand, when a teacher expresses his own ideas, gives directions or criticism, and when he justifies his own use of authority, he will usually be decreasing the freedom of action of students.
> ... the operational definition of direct and indirect influence used in this study is an enumeration of verbal communication within ten categories at continuous intervals of about three seconds by a trained observer.[9]

Hughes, like Flanders, draws on the early theoretical and empirical work of Anderson, Lippit, and White. However, unlike Flanders,

[7] Arno A. Bellack et al., *The Language of the Classroom* (New York: Teachers College Press, 1966), p. 13.

[8] B. Othanel Smith and Milton O. Meux, "A Study of the Logic of Teaching" (Urbana: Bureau of Educational Research, College of Education, University of Illinois, 1963), p. 10.

[9] Ned A. Flanders, "Teacher Influence, Pupil Attitudes, and Achievement: Studies in Interaction Analysis," U.S. Office of Education, Cooperative Research Project No. 397 (Minneapolis: University of Minnesota, 1960), p. 13.

Hughes' category system was not preestablished. Hughes' statement on the development of her category system indicates that her thirty-one categories of teaching functions were abstracted from the data of observation. These thirty-one categories were then combined under seven large categories, whose origins are not identified, but appear to have been at least partially theoretically determined:

> For the purpose of this study, teaching was defined as interaction of teacher with child or group. Through the study of hundreds of episodes of interaction in the teacher-learner situation, thirty-one teaching functions were identified. These functions, with the subscripts that describe how they were performed, form the *Code for the Analysis of Teaching.* It was found that these functions could be placed in seven large categories. [10]

Of all the studies contained in this analysis, the assessment of the development of Taba's category system in relation to her data of observation is the most difficult. Tracing the origins of her category system is difficult for several reasons. Taba's study, of all five, is the least concerned with description for the sake of description. For Taba, description serves the function of producing evidence in a study whose primary concern is the "development of thought": "This study was especially concerned with examining the development of thought under the twin impact of curriculum and teaching strategies designed for an explicit emphasis on cognitive learning." [11] Thus, if the category system was to be functional within the framework of the study's concern, it had to be capable of revealing evidences of the "development of thought." It appears justified to assume that for Taba's category system to have been functional, theoretical limits imposed by the context of the entire study were operative in the origination of the category system. However, unlike Flanders and Hughes, who could draw on the empirical and theoretical concepts of earlier researchers who had studied problems similar to theirs, Taba was developing a category system to identify heretofore unidentified aspects of the teaching enterprise. In a practical sense, she was closer to Smith in having to begin her category system *de novo.* However, she was more limited than Smith by the theoretical constraints and concerns of her study. It is known from Taba's own statement that several category systems were attempted, but she does not indicate whether these attempts were made before or after the data of observation were collected:

---

[10] Marie M. Hughes and Associates, "The Assessment of the Quality of Teaching: A Research Report," U.S. Office of Education Cooperative Research Project No. 353 (Salt Lake City: University of Utah, 1959), p. 288.

[11] Hilda Taba and others, "Thinking in Elementary School Children" (San Francisco: San Francisco State College, 1964), p. 112.

> Several categories of analysis were tried and discarded in the pro-
> cess of experimentation and revision. Among these were the attempts
> to differentiate between different forms, such as questions and state-
> ments, and to identify the errors and fallacies of thought, such as
> appeal to authority, overcautiousness, irrelevance. A similar decision
> was made regarding coding to assess the validity of the content of
> thought. This final coding scheme retained only the distinctions of the
> crudely irrelevant or incorrect statements. [12]

After examining each of these five studies' category systems, one
can suggest a continuum. One terminal point of this continuum may
be defined as a category system arising from the researchers' response
to the data of observation in interaction with a conceptual scheme,
as illustrated by the work of Bellack and Smith. The other terminal
point may be defined as categories already established, as illustrated
by the Flanders study. The category systems developed by Hughes
might be placed close to the Bellack and Smith systems, while that of
Taba might be placed somewhere between the two terminal points.

Whether a category system for curriculum and teaching is most
fruitful when tied to a theoretical system, or most fruitful when as
theoretically unencumbered as possible, cannot as yet be answered
with certainty. However, a category system most free of theoretical
implications might be most useful. A category system derived from
what Conant calls "concepts adequate for description" in a continu-
ous state of refinement, modification, and verification through empirical test and use might serve the field of curriculum and teaching
most effectively.

Having explicated the issues of descriptive theory, theory-as-
hypothesis, and pre-theoretical investigations, a return to a discussion
of the issues raised earlier in the chapter would now seem to be
proper. The place of "prescriptive theory" in the field of curriculum
and teaching can now be examined with more insight because of the
clarification of issues already entertained.

What, then, is the place of "prescriptive theory" in curriculum
and teaching? What is here being suggested as the proper place, if
any, of prescription in curriculum and teaching? The place of prescription in curriculum and teaching is no less important now than it
has always been. Indeed, it is one of the goals of the researcher to
render prescriptive theory eventually more valid and therefore more
valuable. The researcher's job only begins with "concepts adequate
for description" and description itself. The aim of the research is to
produce valid and reliable evidence of relationships or of probable
relationships capable of being translated into if-then terms. For ex-

[12]*Ibid.*, p. 114.

ample: "*If* a pupil has an IQ of 120, *then* he is probably capable of doing college work." It is important here to note that the researcher was said to have as *one* of his goals the rendering of prescription more valid. For the goals of the researcher can be seen as dual: "Historically, the scientific enterprise has been concerned both with knowledge for its own sake and with knowledge for what it can contribute to practical concerns."[13]

The researcher's job, *qua* researcher, is to work toward the specification of relevant variables, their relatedness and interrelatedness which ultimately allows for the prediction of consequences, if only of a statistical or probabilistic order. It is not necessarily the job of researcher-*qua*-researcher to value one set of consequences over another.

Of course, the suggestion that the researcher-*qua*-researcher not involve himself in questions of value is a suggestion to which many researchers take energetic exception. In discussing the relation of evaluation to research, an attempt will be made to explicate the alternative aspects of this issue.

Here it is being suggested that the researcher-*qua*-researcher concern himself with helping to make possible the means necessary to the achievement of goals determined in a wider social context. In addition, he may be asked to provide the evidence with which one will be able to judge the plausibility and probability of alternative sets of prescriptive proposals. Thus it is to be hoped that in the future, when we are asked to accept curriculum proposals whose implementation, we are told, will produce the "democratic man," "the solver of persistent life situations," or "the man who engenders meaning," we might confidently assume that evidence is available to show that the implementation of the prescribed curriculum proposals will indeed yield the prescribed curriculum results.

The above argument in support of the need for research evidence before proposals for curriculum and teaching reforms are instituted is not an attempt to negate the need for or contributions of the educational theorist, philosopher, or prescriber. The researcher-*qua*-researcher should reveal relationships and consequences, not judge them. But the curriculum and teaching enterprise is a valuing one, in which judgments must be made constantly. The need for debate as to what indeed is most worth doing and what is worthwhile is always germane, pertinent, and most crucial. It is no small contribution to suggest what might be the most important values or value in education and to conceptualize the ways in which what is valued might be

[13] Claire Selltiz, Marie Jahoda, Morton Deutsch, Stuart Cook, *Research Methods in Social Relations*, p. 4.

achieved. However, to prescribe actions for which no evidence exists, and for which none is being sought, appears foolhardy. While the researcher-*qua*-researcher has no greater warrant than others for valuing one consequence rather than another, the theorist-*qua*-theorist has no warrant for suggesting that what he values is possible of implementation.

At the outset of this discussion, the first definition of theory suggested was "a set of logically interrelated propositions from which, by deduction, relationships can be demonstrated and new information derived." Then the question was raised as to whether the "stuff" with which the curriculum and teaching researcher and theorist must work is capable of eventually yielding itself to a firm theoretical base. The answer to this question also has several components.

First, it must be affirmed that the curriculum and teaching enterprise, like other practical pursuits of life, exhibits regularities. These regularities can be observed, recorded, conceptualized, analyzed, and related:

> Whether or not the behavior of man as an individual or in a group can be studied scientifically has been discussed for more than a hundred years. The modern way of stating the argument is to ask whether the social sciences are fundamentally different from the natural sciences. My own answer is that there is no basic difference provided one limits the discussion to predictive generalizations based on observation and experiment. [14]

A second aspect of this argument concerns itself with the possibilities of a single science of education with a single theoretical base, about which Conant has this to say:

> Teachers, like physicians, think in terms of predictive generalizations as well as arguments derived from general principles. Some people would like to combine these two modes of thought and speak of a single all-embracing science of education. The question is whether it is useful to try to cover with the word "science" a vast field of human activity directed toward practical ends. I have come to the conclusion that it is not. Perhaps it is only a question of terminology. However, I prefer not to speak of the science of engineering but of the engineering sciences. I doubt that there is or ever will be a science of medicine, yet I am sure enormous strides forward have been made in the medical sciences. Therefore, I think it would be better to discuss the academic disciplines that have relevance for the labors of the teacher than to talk in terms of developing a science of education. In other words, I shall examine academic disciplines which might be called educational sciences or educational disciplines, rather than the science of the discipline of education. [15]

[14] James B. Conant, *The Education of American Teachers* (New York: McGraw-Hill Book Co., 1963), p. 117.
[15] *Ibid.*, p. 117.

A position exactly opposite to Conant's is expressed by McMurray:

> This does not mean that educators are totally without resources. Nor does it mean that the few facts available, plus the greater bulk of theory are to be spurned by educators merely because of their limited validity. Whatever we have should be used. But the separateness of the foundation disciplines makes it exceedingly difficult to find their potential significance for an internally consistent solution to the problems of education. What is most required is a discipline standing between the basic sciences on the one hand and practical pedagogy on the other. Such a discipline must be theoretical, and it must reflect the sophisticated theoretical domains concerning personality formation, learning, social change, institutional process, cognition, esthetic apprehension, and so on. It would be impossible to blend such a diversity of raw materials unless the educational theorist at the same time constructed his own basic concepts by which to judge relevance and coherence. Furthermore, no matter how freely he might borrow theoretic instruments from social sciences, his educational discipline must be an independent theory, such that it can be examined in its own right rather than by a multitude of backward references. If this were not the case, then an eclectic heaping together of theoretical and largely speculative materials would reduce the probable validity of the outcome to a point well below the degree of credence we demand as a basis for deliberate action upon human beings. [16]

The position being suggested here on this issue is, in a sense, a compromise between the unified theory approach and the discipline of education approach. Before suggestions for explanations are appropriate, knowledge of the phenomena is necessary. Discussions of *why* must follow a knowledge of *what*. It is the job of the curriculum and teaching researcher to know, through observation and description, of what the classroom enterprise is composed. Theoretical explanations as to *why* must follow a knowledge of *what*. Explanations as to *why* must follow after observation and descriptions have been categorized. It is at the why stage that the accumulated knowledge and training of academicians and other professionals must be tapped if meaningful explanations for complex phenomena are to be hypothesized. For this reason the suggestion was made earlier that the category systems themselves be as free from theoretical encumbrances as possible. A category system in the area of curriculum and teaching will be most useful if it can be manipulated in many different theoretical frameworks. The insight gained from close association with academicians and other professionals will permit the curriculum and teaching researcher to conduct experimentation that will affirm or deny insights developed through the interplay of his own detailed knowledge and the knowledge of practitioners in the disciplines and

[16] Foster McMurray, "Preface to an Autonomous Discipline of Education," *Educational Theory*, 5:135, July, 1955.

the professions. It may be pertinent to note here that some highly valued clues for the teaching of the neurologically impaired were derived from the work of an optometrist. Thus, it is suggested that the curriculum and teaching researcher begin with classroom observation, description, and categorization. His next move, toward explanation, should be undertaken with the theoretical and practical help of the academicians and other professionals. This path will render his resulting classroom experimental research more accurate, more sophisticated, and more significant.

IV

The Relation of Individuality of Definition to Communicability

Science is social, an activity of the group rather than an isolated independent enterprise. A scientific structure can be built or created by many investigators and extensively developed branches of science are all joint enterprises. The cooperative nature of scientific research accounts for the "objectivity" of science. The data with which scientists deal are public data, available to a qualified investigator who makes the appropriate observations. Scientists in reporting their experiments include a wealth of detail, not for its own intrinsic interest but to enable any other investigator to duplicate the experimental setup and thus see for himself whether the reported result really does occur. There are many cases in which individuals are mistaken in what they think they see, in a court of law witnesses will swear to conflicting versions of events at which both were present, with no intentional perjury on the part of either. Many times men will see what they expect, or what they want to see, rather than what actually occurs, although the facts of experience are the ultimate court of appeal for scientists, there must be public facts which everyone can experience under appropriate conditions. When elaborate experiments are repeated by various different scientists again and again it does not token suspicion or distrust of the other man's results, but universal agreement that to be decisive facts must be public and repeatable. Repetition and careful checking by qualified observers minimize the intrusion of subjective factors and help maintain the objectivity of science.[1]

If a community of persons interested in the same field share a common theoretical perspective and vocabulary, then communication is rendered efficient and easy. In fields where key terms have agreed-upon referents, research findings and theoretical constructs are easily communicated, discussed, criticized, and utilized. In other fields, each researcher is free to construct or reconstruct his own unique definitions or system of definitions. Thus, accurate communi-

[1] Irving M. Copi, *Introduction to Logic*, 2nd ed. (New York: The Macmillan Co., 1961), p. 415.

cation depends upon the willingness of tne receivers of information to first encode novel definitions or definition systems before approaching new ideas and research findings. This, of course, cannot help but impair the quality, quantity, and speed of interfield communication. However, the problem of the proliferation of unique definition systems is a concomitant of the existence of competing, conflicting, and contrasting conceptual frameworks. In fields where the latter is found, so also is the former. The existence of several definitions for the same terms is a problem common in the social sciences, and so also is the resulting problem of impaired communication. The concept of "role" common to the literature of the social sciences is an example of just such an embarrassment of riches of definition. So many and varied are the definitions of "role" that Neal Gross, in his *Explorations in Role Analysis*, is able to identify three categories of definition, and to state further that these three categories do not exhaust the suggested definitions of the term:

> Of several possible categories into which definitions of the term "role" might be placed, we have selected and will examine three, which if not exhaustive, are at least representative of the major role formulations in the social science literature.
>
> Definitions of role which either equate it with or define it to include *normative culture patterns* have been placed in the first category.[2]
>
> In some definitions a role is treated as an *individual's definition of his situation with reference to his and others' social position*, and these deserve a separate categorization.[3]
>
> In a third category we would place definitions which deal with role as *the behavior of actors occupying social positions.*[4]

Those who work in the field of curriculum and teaching are similarly plagued by a plethora of definitions for very major term: teacher, learner, curriculum, and so on. Because the five studies here analyzed do not exhibit theoretical congruency, there is no single term that all these investigators define. Some terms are described, while others are defined. In those cases in which the same term is defined by at least two researchers, they are generally defined differently. Thus, while Hughes defines teaching in one sense, Smith defines it in an entirely different sense. Hughes writes:

> However, a description of teaching as it was in progress in the classroom could be secured by defining "teaching as interaction." Interaction is used in its dictionary sense of mutual or reciprocal action or

[2] Neal Gross, Ward S. Mason, and Alexander W. McEachern, *Explorations in Role Analysis* (New York: John Wiley and Sons, 1958), p. 11.

[3] *Ibid.*, p. 13.

[4] *Ibid.*, p. 14.

influence. In other words the partner or objects in a situation act upon each other. Teaching, therefore, cannot be separated from the learner.[5]

For purposes of the study, teaching was defined as interaction in the teacher-learner situation of the classroom and school where the adult holds the position of teacher in relationship to the child.[6]

However, Smith asserts:

That learning does not necessarily issue from teaching, that teaching is one thing and learning is quite another is significant for pedagogical research.[7]

Smith defines teaching's essential features:

In its essential features it is a system of social action involving an agent, an end-in-view, a situation and two sets of factors in the situation—one set over which the agent has no control and one set which the agent can modify with respect to the end-in-view.[8]

The impaired communicability resulting from the uniqueness of definition seems inherent in the curriculum and teaching research enterprise at this stage of its development. It is, wrote Aristotle, the mark of an educated man to expect no more exactness than the subject permits. To expect a unitary system of definitions in a field not yet described is to expect a rigor that would doubtlessly stultify research formulation and theoretical constructs. However, it is difficult to deny that this freedom of definition exacts a price. In all fields in which idiosyncratic definitions are found, communication is lessened, but in the field of curriculum and teaching, the problem is further compounded by both the nature of the training of teachers and the nature of the teaching enterprise. When research findings are disseminated among sociologists and psychologists, for example, it is assumed that communication is within a community of persons trained to interpret, analyze, and evaluate research findings. That the sophistication of the reader mitigates the confusion caused by the existence of conflicting cognitive frameworks and unique definition systems is the assumption of the communicant.

In the field of curriculum and teaching, no such assumption is possible. Teachers are not trained to read, interpret, and evaluate

[5] Marie M. Hughes, "The Utah Study of the Assessment of Teaching," in Arno A. Bellack, ed., *Theory and Research in Teaching* (New York: Bureau of Publications, Teachers College, Columbia University, 1963), p. 27.

[6] Marie M. Hughes and Associates, "The Assessment of the Quality of Teaching: A Research Report," U.S. Office of Education Cooperative Research Project No. 353 (Salt Lake City: University of Utah, 1959), p. 11.

[7] B. Othanel Smith, "A Concept of Teaching," *Teachers College Record*, 61:233, February, 1960.

[8] B. Othanel Smith and Milton O. Meux, "A Study of the Logic of Teaching" (Urbana: Bureau of Educational Research, College of Education, University of Illinois, 1963), p. 3.

research findings. However, the nature of the teaching task is so vast, complex, and problem-filled that teachers quite legitimately seek to understand and make use of the information derived from research. That much of the research so far completed does not lend itself to immediate classroom application is yet another aspect of this problem that serves to further aggravate the situation. Thus, on the one hand, research findings are difficult to read, understand, analyze, interpret, and utilize. On the other hand, the increasing societal demands on the teacher vastly increase the teacher's demand for usable information.

Situations similar to this have occurred in the past and were met by the emergence of the middleman, the interpreter of theory and research. While fulfilling a function, the interpreter often biases theoretical constructs and research findings through his own process of selection, emphasis, and interpretation. Often the interpreter is himself poorly trained in theory, empirical methods of investigation, and statistics. Thus superimposed on a field already fragmentized by differing conceptual frameworks and idiosyncratic definitions are both accurate and erroneous interpretations of these same frameworks and definitions. Often these same interpreters urge the translation into practice of research findings without sufficient caution:

> This detachment is peculiarly hard to secure in the case of those persons who are concerned with building up the scientific content of educational practices and arts. There is a pressure for immediate results, for a demonstration of a quick short span of usefulness in school. There is a tendency to convert the results of statistical inquiries and laboratory experiments into directions and rules for the conduct of school administration and instruction. Results tend to be directly grabbed, as it were, and put into operation by teachers. Then there is not the leisure for that slow gradual independent growth of theories that is the necessary condition of the formation of a true science.[9]

How then is open and individualized research practice, so necessary in an infant field, maintained without depriving teachers, supervisors, and administrators of needed information while still protecting them from the dissemination of faulty or biased reporting? The most effective way to accomplish this, but the least productive of immediate results, would be to enlarge the education of teachers to include those areas of knowledge necessary to an adequate understanding of research and theory. This practice would enable the teacher to interpret research without mediation. To alleviate the problem in a more immediate sense several steps may be taken. It would seem judicious to continue the practices that presently pro-

[9] John Dewey, *The Sources of a Science of Education* (New York: Horace Liveright, 1929), p. 17.

mote accurate communication, terminate those practices that hinder communication, and institute some new practices that might promote better communication.

Teachers, supervisors, and administrators have long accepted the practice of workshops, colloquiums, conferences, and in-service training. For those teachers, supervisors, and administrators in the field who are interested in developing a background that would enable them to profit from the reading of research material, in-service courses might be designed to accomplish this end. For others not so well motivated, hearing reports at workshops, colloquiums, and conventions on the state of research by those involved in it might further the cultivation of a more knowledgeable research audience. Researchers cannot restrict interpretations of their work, but they can assay the educational literature and enter disclaimers when they feel they have been grossly misinterpreted.

Within the context of the research report itself, much can be done to promote clarity of communication. Although definitions are free to be both unique and stipulative, their usefulness is enhanced when they are, as Scheffler suggests: ". . . formally coherent and pragmatically well-chosen."[10]

In what is otherwise the most readable of all five reports, Marie Hughes introduces a novel stipulative definition of "content" that cannot fail to hinder communication. While Scheffler maintains that one may not fault a stipulative definition for failure to reflect a term's normal meaning, he nevertheless maintains that stipulative definitions should not arouse *unwanted associations*. When, therefore, Hughes defines content development, a term in constant and agreed-upon use in educational literature, as ". . . response to the data placed in the situation by the children,"[11] she cannot fail to arouse those *unwanted associations* and thus diminish communication. Therefore, while individuality of conceptual frameworks and systems of definition have here been seen as proper to the present state of research in teaching, researchers should be urged to abide by Scheffler's injunction to use definitions that are both formally coherent and pragmatically well chosen and to avoid stipulative definitions that arouse unwanted associations.

[10] Israel Scheffler, *The Language of Education* (Springfield, Illinois: Charles C Thomas, 1960), p. 15.
[11] Marie M. Hughes and Associates, "The Assessment of the Quality of Teaching," p. 69.

V

The Researcher and Prescriptions for Behavior

In Chapter III it was suggested that the most useful category system may be that system with the least theoretical encumbrances, for the ability to manipulate categories of description in many different theoretical frameworks is enhanced when categories are as free as possible of theoretical attachments. If the category system can be manipulated in different theoretical frameworks, then the complex nature of the teaching enterprise may be more easily revealed.

Few people who write of curriculum and teaching deny the need for explanations of classroom behavior that derive from knowledge from many different fields and professions. Even those who believe that the field of curriculum and teaching can be adequately explained in terms of one central focus, be it psychological, anthropological, political, or other, are challenged seriatim by all the other unidimensional explanations that chose a different single focus. In interpreting both the position of those who see the need for multidimensional interpretation and those who suggest there is a central factor that can explain all, and then proceed to disagree upon what that central factor is, one is forced to conclude that, at least for the present, identification of a central explanatory factor is not possible or profitable. The category system that is most adaptable for use in multidimensional interpretation is both most practical and most profitable. There appears to be another significant advantage to be gained in the development of the unencumbered category system, the advantage of longevity. The development of a viable, reliable, and valid category system for classroom behavior, although often lightly esteemed, is a difficult and arduous effort. If the category system is entwined in a hypothetical-theoretical system, it will remain viable and valid (its reliability non-pertinent) only so long as that hypothetical-theoretical system from which it derives is held to be valid.

Since such systems of explanation come to pass and pass away not too rarely in curriculum and teaching, if category systems are irrevocably committed to one or another theoretical point of view, then the field will periodically be forced to begin again. So the theoretically free category system may help solve the problem of retaining the benefits of vast amounts of intellectual effort.

The problem of the relation of evaluation to research may be viewed as closely related to the problems discussed above. The establishment of category systems that tie in evaluative terms, ideas, and positions cannot do other than lead to the same kind of difficulties as those that result from encumbering a category system with theoretical commitments. Indeed, the interlarding of evaluation with category systems may be even more pernicious and costly.

Arguments as to what is the good, the true, and the beautiful date back to the beginning of recorded history. If little else has been learned, certainly one fact seems clear—there is no general agreement as to what constitutes the good, the true, and the beautiful. Similarly, there is no agreement as to what constitutes the good, the true, and the beautiful in curriculum and teaching, although workers in the field cling to the notion that not only is agreement possible but obvious.

> Most classroom visitors go to the classroom with definite preconceptions of what they are looking for. They go to the classroom not to find out what effective behavior is, but to see whether the teacher is behaving effectively, i.e., the way they believe he should behave.
>
> Most such attempts have used ratings on *a priori* dimensions believed to be related to effectiveness. Such rating approaches have been uniformly unsuccessful in yielding measures of teaching skill. No fallacy is more widely believed than the one which says it is possible to judge a teacher's skill by watching him teach. It is difficult to find anyone, professional educator or layman, who does not think he himself, at least, can recognize good teaching when he sees it.[1]

There are valuing concepts which often appear so very obvious and good to the holder of the concept that it is inconceivable that differing and conflicting positions may exist. Illustrations from some of the studies being investigated may help to demonstrate various aspects of this problem, and indicate how complex this problem can be.

Flanders has two major concepts that he uses to analyze teacher influence—direct and indirect teacher influence:

> *Direct influence* by a teacher restricts the freedom of a student by setting restraints or focusing his attention on an idea.

---

[1] Donald Medley and Harold E. Mitzel, "Measuring Classroom Behavior by Systematic Observation," in N. L. Gage, ed., *Handbook of Research on Teaching* (Chicago: Rand McNally Co., 1963), p. 257.

> *Indirect influence* by a teacher increases the freedom of action of a student by reducing restraints or encouraging participation.[2]

It does not seem possible to deny that the word "freedom" in our society delivers a strong, positive message. It seems, therefore, quite logical to wish to increase, rather than restrict, what is so positive. When one looks at Flanders' definition of what restriction of freedom entails, one might well wonder if this "restriction," as defined by Flanders, is not an important positive aspect of the adult's relationship to the child. To cite an obvious example: If child A is about to hit child B, and the teacher stops child A, then child A's freedom is restricted, but may we not say that child B's freedom (from hurt, injustice, and so on) has been expanded? If one looks at the second half of Flanders' definition of freedom restriction, he learns that freedom is restricted when a teacher attempts to focus a child's attention on an idea. Taba, in using the very same concept of "focus," treats focusing as an important aspect of teaching strategies in thinking. Thus, to Taba, attempting to focus the child's attention is either a neutral or a positive act, but nowhere does she indicate that she considers it negative:

> Focusing establishes both the topic and the particular cognitive operation to be performed. It sets the cognitive task. For example, the question by the teacher, "If the desert had all the water it needed what would happen?" establishes the central focus for discussion and calls for prediction of consequences.
> The coding system also specifies the shifts in subject matter (change of focus), the degree to which the teacher finds it necessary to bring the discussion back to the original topic (refocus) and the number of times that the discussion wanders from the subject (deviation from focus).[3]

Thus, one of the two aspects that Flanders uses to define his negative valued central concept, direct influence, focusing student's attention on an idea, is described in Taba's study as a neutral or somewhat positive component of teaching.

In a further explanation of his position, Flanders states: "There are many different ways to increase or decrease the number of alternatives for action available to the students. The smaller work-group with a student chairman is less subject to the restraints of teacher control than is the total class with the teacher in charge."[4] Are we being asked to believe that student authority over students is more beneficial and on what grounds?

[2] Ned A. Flanders, "Teacher Influence, Pupil Attitudes, and Achievement: Studies in Interaction Analysis," U.S. Office of Education Cooperative Research Project No. 397 (Minneapolis: University of Minnesota, 1960), p. 12.

[3] Hilda Taba and others, "Thinking in Elementary School Children" (San Francisco: San Francisco State College, 1964), p. 120.

[4] Ned A. Flanders, "Teacher Influence, Pupil Attitudes, and Achievement," p. 12.

Hughes, in analyzing teacher behavior, uses the twin concepts of teacher power and teacher responsiveness. Hughes' concepts are quite close to Flanders' notion of direct and indirect influence. Hughes, like Flanders, believes that teacher influence, power, and authority exist, and that the good teacher acts to reduce this influence, power, and authority. Writes Hughes:

> A definition of good teaching, within our framework of functions performed in the classroom, requires a *reduction* in the number of Controlling Functions performed. The power component of the teacher should be ameliorated with the overt statement (Public Criteria) of the reason for a direction or command.[5]

Hannah Arendt, in discussing *The Crisis in Education*, deals with the concept of teacher-child and parent-child authority and has a far different view from the one indicated by both Flanders and Hughes:

> In education, on the contrary, there can be no such ambiguity in regard to the present-day loss of authority. Children cannot throw off educational authority as though they were in a position of oppression by an adult majority—though even this absurdity of treating children as an oppressed minority in need of liberation has actually been tried out in modern educational practice. Authority has been discarded by the adults, and this can mean only one thing: that the adults refuse to assume responsibility for the world into which they have brought the children.[6]

Arendt concludes her essay in much the same vein:

> What concerns us all and cannot therefore be turned over to the special science of pedagogy is the relation between grown-ups and children in general, or, putting it in even more general and exact terms, our attitude toward the fact of natality; the fact that we have all come into the world by being born and that this world is constantly renewed through birth. Education is the point at which we decide whether we love the world enough to assume responsibility for it and by the same token save it from that ruin which, except for renewal, except for the coming of the new and young, would be inevitable. And education, too, is where we decide whether we love our children enough not to expel them from our world and leave them to their own devices, nor to strike from their hands their chance of undertaking something new, something unforeseen by us, but to prepare them in advance for the task of renewing a common world.[7]

In using these illustrations, the attempt was neither to adjudicate the above stated differences nor to espouse one position rather than another, but rather to urge a greater degree of sophistication in deal-

[5] Marie M. Hughes and Associates, "The Assessment of the Quality of Teaching: A Research Report," U.S. Office of Education Cooperative Research Project No. 353 (Salt Lake City: University of Utah, 1959), p. 295.

[6] Hannah Arendt, *Between Past and Future* (New York: The Viking Press, 1961), p. 190.

[7] *Ibid.*, p. 196.

ing with valuing. There is indeed no one way of viewing, and thus valuing, a given act, attitude, or situation. And so when the researcher-*qua*-researcher promotes one value position rather than another, indeed when he weaves these values into his category system, he is inviting valuing arguments.

Because valuing arguments have a long and noble history of remaining unsolved, there are those who maintain that the continuation of these arguments is of little worth. That position is definitely not being upheld here. The nature of teaching and curriculum as a human enterprise in which valuing is central has already been asserted. It is simply that valuing and research represent two entirely different enterprises. Valuing may be viewed as largely noncumulative, while it is in the very nature of any activity deemed scientific to be both cumulative and progressive. Kuhn asks: "Does a field make progress because it is a science, or is it a science because it makes progress?"[8]

To mix evaluation with research is to benefit neither enterprise. Evaluative decisions can be made most effectively after as many facts as possible, gathered through research, have been revealed. When evaluation has to be separated from facts before thoughtful judgments can be made, the entire evaluative enterprise is rendered more difficult. The fostering of research accumulation will be impaired if valuing arguments accompany research premises, category systems, and conclusions.

Of all five category systems, the Bellack system is the one least evaluative and most neutral. The Smith and Taba studies represent two different kinds of evaluative problems. Taba hypothesizes the good, and designs a study to accomplish it. Smith claims to be reporting a neutral study:

> The study reported herein is neither an evaluative nor an experimental investigation of teaching. No attempt is made to determine the effects of teaching behavior on students. Nor is there an attempt to establish correlations among variables or to search for causes of teacher behavior. Rather, this study is an analytic and descriptive one in the natural history sense. An effort is made to develop a way of dividing verbal teaching behavior into pedagogically significant units, and to analyze the units in logically meaningful ways.[9]

Yet even before making the above assertion, in which he states that his aim is analysis and description, Smith has already, five pages

[8] T. Kuhn, *The Structure of Scientific Revolutions* (Chicago: University of Chicago Press, 1962), p. 161.

[9] B. Othanel Smith and Milton O. Meux, "A Study of the Logic of Teaching" (Urbana: Bureau of Educational Research, College of Education, University of Illinois, 1963), p. 8.

earlier, established an arbitrary criterion, measured teachers against the criterion, and found them wanting:

> By "logical operations," which are the focus of our study, we mean the forms which verbal behavior takes as the teacher shapes the subject matter in the course of instruction. For example, the teacher reduces concepts to linguistic patterns called definitions; he fills in gaps between the student's experience and some new phenomena by facts and generalizations related in a verbal pattern referred to as explanation; he rates objects, events, etc. by reference to facts and criteria related in a pattern called evaluation. If he does not engage in such operations himself, the teacher either requires his students to do so, or, more typically, the teacher and his students jointly carry on these operations through verbal exchanges.
>
> These operations exhibit a structure which can be observed and described. Of course, the structure as it is exhibited in the classroom is often incomplete because the operation is formed elliptically. The teacher may not follow exactly the pattern of a particular type of definition or the complete outlines of a particular form of explanation. Nevertheless, these operations are clearly enough outlined in teaching behavior to be identified and described.
>
> Moreover, these operations can be evaluated logically by reference to rules of validity and correctness, and while such rules do not describe how a given operation is to be performed, they do afford checking points as to the clarity and rigor of the operation's performance. When teaching behavior takes the form of operations whose pattern can be evaluated by reference to rules of validity and correctness, it is said to be logical. [10]

While, on the one hand, Smith disclaims any intention of valuing, he chooses to describe certain verbal teaching practices as belonging to the realm of logic. Having thus identified them as belonging in that realm, he then further identifies these verbal practices as poor exemplars of logical classes. Had Smith begun by calling the verbal teaching practices he found in the school "para-defining," "semiconditional inferring," or "D23," he might have avoided the entire problem. For once Smith takes the position that while teachers perform "logical operations" they perform them "elliptically," he is then pushed further into that uncertain realm of judgment and speculation by then having to deal with the meaning of this "ellipticalness." So Smith speculates:

> It is interesting to speculate briefly about the role of rules in teaching. The teacher's authority for saying that a student's response is either correct or incorrect has traditionally rested largely upon what the textbook says. This practice has been decried as enslaving the student and the teacher intellectually, as thwarting initiative and creativity, and as emphasizing memorization in learning. If this practice is to be abandoned, it would seem that the teacher must learn to understand and

[10] *Ibid.*, p. 3

control the logical operations which he and his students perform. The responses given by the student are correct because of what the book says or they are correct on logical grounds. Of course, they may be correct on both counts. But the teacher who is able to move about logically in a network of ideas and to monitor the performance of logical operations would appear to be free, in large measure, from enslavement to the text. To monitor such performance the teacher must have recourse to the rules by which logical operations may be evaluated. To be sure it is not necessary that the teacher be constantly aware of the rules which he is using as he evaluates the performance of logical operations in the classroom. But he should be able to refer to such rules when the need for doing so arises. [11]

And so we now learn from Smith's speculation that, if teachers had better control of those same "logical operations" Smith identified earlier as being performed elliptically, the teacher would be less enslaved by the textbook. Space does not permit a full analysis of Smith's speculations, but perhaps several points may be raised. The dictionary defines logic as:

1. The science that deals with the canons and criteria of validity in thought and demonstration; the science of the formal principles of reasoning. 2. A treatise on this science; also, the methodology or formal principles of any branch of knowledge; as, the logic of art. 3. Reasoning; esp. sound reasoning; also, ironically whatever convinces or makes argument useless; as, artillery has been called the logic of kings. 4. Connection, as of facts or events, in a rational way; as, by the logic of events, anarchy leads to tyranny. [12]

If one accepts any of the above definitions of logic, it is difficult to see from which textbooks teachers will be freed, even if they were in control of logical operations. One might hopefully be able to evaluate the arguments or evidence contained in textbooks more validly if one were in control of "logical operations," but in what way would this mitigate the reliance on texts in mathematics, science, music, grammar, and literature? Logic might be an aid in evaluating positions advanced in the social studies, but not in the establishment of historical facts to which rules other than logic apply. Perhaps the most novel idea Smith presents is the ability of control of "logical operations" to free initiative and creativity. While one might with some effort accept that a knowledge of logic might free initiative, to think of a knowledge of logic as freeing creativity requires more effort than can be mustered here. Logic's chief characteristic is rigor, and rigor suggests all its synonyms: strictness, stiffness, rigidity, and severity. All these characteristics seem the very

---

[11] *Ibid.*, p. 60.
[12] *Webster's New Collegiate Dictionary* (Springfield, Mass.: G. and C. Merriam Co., 1961), p. 495.

antithesis of creativity. One wonders how Smith was able to suggest logic as freeing creativity, unless Smith's definition of creativity is an unusual one. Perhaps, had Smith developed this point more fully, the reader may have been better able to follow Smith's reasoning.

If one had accepted Smith's original judgment of teachers' verbal activity as generally elliptical, based on standards of formal logic, one of the conclusions of Smith's "A Study of the Logic of Teaching" might have seemed incongruous:

> Logic could be broadened in two ways: one would be the investigation of logical operations as they appear in ordinary language, operations such as defining, describing, and explaining; the other would be the comparative investigation of patterns of reasoning and argument used in various fields such as mathematics, physics, biology, law, ethics, and esthetics. A trend toward such a broadened conception of logic is illustrated in the works of Toulmin, Jeusen, and Hart and Honore.
>
> Such a conception of logic would be helpful in identifying more accurately the kinds of logical operations that occur in the classroom. It would also help us by providing a greater variety of logical forms—e.g., kinds of argument used in everyday life—that we could use as standards to assess classroom discourse. [13]

And so Smith, having already assessed classroom discourse against standards of current logic and found classroom discourse insufficiently logical, concludes his study by telling us that present logic is insufficiently broad, and a broader logic would offer a different and superior standard against which to measure classroom discourse. Perhaps the discovery of the classroom logic is what is needed, so that standards of legitimacy of classroom discourse may be established that are independent of formal logic or everyday logic and are related to the nature of the classroom enterprise.

The relation of evaluation to Taba's study is much more obvious, but no less complex. Taba's entire study has large evaluative components. Her central objective, to examine the development of thought under optimal training conditions, is itself an evaluative statement. It is evaluative because it asserts the study will provide "optimal training conditions" and that those training conditions are superior to others. Evidence to the truth of these facts is not given, so that one is asked to agree to a judgment. Taba's conceptual scheme is based on her interpretation of Piaget's work and could not be challenged in the sense that no personal interpretation is challengeable. However, one cannot be asked to accept the results of this study as in any way replicating, extending, challenging, or repudiating Piaget's work. This aspect of Taba's study will be discussed in greater detail later, as will other specific aspects. The entire Taba study, from teacher selection

[13] B. Othanel Smith and Milton O. Meux, "A Study of the Logic of Teaching," p. 196.

through teacher training, evaluation of growth, and ending in a category system for analyzing teacher strategies, is based on questionable judgments. Indeed, one judgment builds upon another in a, to use a Taba term, hierarchical pattern, so that if one cannot agree to the initial judgments, the results of the entire study are in question. Indeed, if one cannot agree to the major but unstated premise that children's thinking can be reliably and validly measured through their participation in classroom discourse and through their responses to the Social Studies Inference Test, one also will have difficulty in accepting all other aspects of the study.

Until now, in discussing the relation of evaluation to research, the problem has been viewed as existing between the researcher and his stance toward evaluation, and it has been suggested over and over again that the researcher serves both the research and the valuing enterprise best by keeping his research free from evaluation and thus more usable, cumulative, and lasting. However, there is another aspect to this issue which must be elucidated, and that is the criteria for evaluating research itself. Research is to be valued in terms of the reliability, validity, and fruitfulness of its findings. The researcher's status, stature, or eminence is entirely irrelevant in evaluating the merits of the research, which must be evaluated in terms of the clarity of its concepts and the usefulness or potential usefulness of its findings.

Earlier in the study when the suggestion was made that the re-searcher-*qua*-researcher not involve himself with questions of valuing, it was noted that some researchers would take energetic exception to that suggestion. It is often argued that one can legitimately urge the change of certain teaching practices on the basis of incomplete research evidence, for the teaching practices currently in use are based on no research. This position is not being supported here for two reasons. At the very minimum, current practices allow the enterprise to take place. Although no research findings undergird these practices, they have evolved from years of practical experience in classroom teaching. Evidence that a specific change is possible and has the effect predicted and desired should be conclusive before widespread change is advocated.

The second reason for not supporting those who urge change on the basis of incomplete evidence derives from the complex nature of the teaching enterprise. Common practices in teaching, as in other human enterprises, often serve functions that are not immediately apparent. Thus, in addition to the manifest function a practice obviously serves, Merton speaks of latent functions that common practices also discharge. For example, schooling may be seen as serving the function of educating the young. An examination of schooling at other levels may reveal that other functions, latent functions, are served by this enterprise: limiting the labor supply, freeing parents of custodial care, raising the marriage age and thus lowering the birth rate. Often it is not until a change in patterns occurs that one can identify what latent functions were served by former patterns. For example, with the passing of the small towns and the growth of the more anonymous urban and suburban areas, practices associated with small-town life are being reevaluated. Gossip, once viewed as a time passer for idlers, might also be viewed as a highly effective, informal device for social control. When change takes place spontaneously, one must deal with the resulting problems as best one can.

However, when change is suggested and planned for, one must have as complete a knowledge as possible of the ensuing consequences. If one can accept the validity of the latent function concept, it suggests the need for great care before introducing change. It is necessary to know why certain teaching practices prevail, as well as to identify that they do. It is necessary to ascertain what functions the patterns in practice serve before suggesting they be discarded. It is further necessary to know whether or not the suggested practices will discharge the same latent functions the older practices discharged, in cases where the fulfillment of these latent functions is still valued. To move from the identification of practices, to the valuing of these practices, to the replacement of these same practices with others, appears to be insufficiently cautious. The stage of identification and description should be followed by explanation. It is necessary to know why a practice has been in use before a substitute is offered for it. If each succeeding practice does not at least attempt to fulfill the necessary functions the former practice was effectively serving, researchers will be constantly causing at least as many problems as they solve. Before we urge, for example, all teachers to reduce their power or authority component, we must establish what aspects of the teaching enterprise are being well served or disserved by teachers functioning as they do.

VI

Relationships between Researcher and Teacher, Administrator and Supervisor

In Chapter IV individuality of definition and its relation to communicability were discussed. Reference was made to the need for teachers to be more sophisticated readers of research, and some ways to achieve this end were suggested. In a very real sense, this issue is as much an aspect of the question now presented, the relationship of the researcher to the teacher, as it is an aspect of the question of the nature of individuality of definition and its relation to communicability. It might be helpful to restate, expand, and further explore some statements about the issue of communicability. It is again suggested that teachers be trained to read and understand research findings, thus eventually obviating the need for interpreters of research. While it was suggested that the present state of research in teaching necessitates the existence of unique patterns of definition and idiosyncratic conceptual frameworks, that this causes great loss of communicability seems obvious. Realizing that communication is difficult at present, the researcher should endeavor to enhance communication where possible, so that teachers, administrators, and supervisors will be encouraged to make the effort to read original work. One way to enhance readability is to utilize some agreed-upon form in reporting findings. Idiosyncratic forms of reporting research, while understandable in the past, will serve no other end than confusion if continued into the future. The incongruency of structure that characterizes these studies puts a burden on the reader, be he researcher, teacher, supervisor, or administrator. For when a field is characterized by new beginnings, codification of any aspect is impossible. When, however, a community of persons of similar interest emerges, the establishment of "rules of the game" is possible.

Just as the answer to the second general question has aspects that overlap into a discussion of the relations between researcher, teacher, administrator, and supervisor, the answer to the third general question leads directly to the nature of the relationship between the researcher and others. For even when the researcher attempts a scrupulous division between observation and judgment and prescription, he often carries with him the perspective that derives from the historical fact of classroom research's beginnings:

> Direct observation of classroom behavior was first used in research on teaching effectiveness, and it has been used, and misused, most often in such research. Teacher effectiveness must ultimately be defined in terms of effects on pupils, in terms, more specifically, of changes in pupil behavior, but it is widely believed that a trained supervisor or expert of some type can assess the effectiveness of a teacher by watching him teach. It is safe to say that most of the many studies relating one variable to another to teacher effectiveness have used some such judgment as a criterion of teacher effectiveness.[1]

Research into classroom behavior was originally viewed as an attempt to find an accurate, reliable, and valid measure of teacher effectiveness, and the goal of the research was to render the supervisor's job more efficient. Just as the department store president could, by surveying statements of profit and loss, determine his most efficient department, so, it was hoped, the school supervisor or administrator could, if only the right instrument were found, determine his most efficient classroom and classroom teacher.

It would be as if the primary concern of research in medicine was to devise a scale for the rating of doctors. It is generally agreed that even if the goal of predictive generalizations in classroom behavior were achieved, the generalizations would be of a statistical and probabilistic nature. This being the case, could *one* individual supervisor in *one* school rate *one* teacher by the use of a rating scale whose nature is probabilistic without running the risk of committing a grave injustice? For example, the Flanders study is the only one of the five studies reported here that shows a correlation between one type of teaching, indirect, and higher student achievement. However, as Flanders himself points out, this superior student achievement is a mean difference and does not indicate that every class taught by a teacher whose pattern of teaching was indirect achieved more than each class taught by a teacher whose pattern of teaching was direct.

[1] Donald Medley and Harold E. Mitzel, "Measuring Classroom Behavior by Systematic Observation," in N. L. Gage, ed., American Educational Research Association Handbook of Research on Teaching (Chicago: Rand-McNally, 1963), p. 248.

The classroom researcher should expend his energies in explicating the classroom enterprise, hopefully to render the enterprise more predictable and thus more controllable. Research into classroom behavior cannot go forward without the support of teachers, supervisors, and administrators. It is likely that the support will be more freely given when the researcher is viewed by the profession as independent of such issues as teacher evaluation, merit pay, and promotions of any kind.

The aim of the curriculum and teaching researcher should be the development of analytic tools to be put at the disposal of the clinician to render the clinic situation more successful and more predictable. There is a vast and complex job to be done, and the job grows increasingly more vast and more complex. Until now, teaching appears to have gone forward by a combination of intuition, guesswork, and the ability of the older generation of teachers to pass on the secrets of the trade to the younger. This system has worked well enough in the past. However, the schools are now being asked to educate to a high level of competence children who by every standard of evidence have not been prepared by home and the larger environment for the student role, and who operate from an emotional and mental set that is often foreign to that of their teachers. In the not too distant past, those who did not find a sympathetic environment in school could leave at a relatively young age and find a more benign environment elsewhere. Within our presently evolving technological society, there are increasingly less opportunities for a satisfactory life for those who fail at school. Thus, school errors are increasingly costly to the individual, the school, and to the society. To increase the area of knowledge about school life, and thus hopefully eventually to reduce the area of possible error, is the task of the researcher that is being proposed here.

VII

Curriculum and Teaching Area Sampled by Each Study

It seems a happy accident that when one inspects the total classroom sampling of these five studies, as shown in Table I, one finds that these studies as a group have some sample of classroom behavior from all school grades, kindergarten through twelfth grade. Although the exact number of hours of classroom observations is not given by each researcher, one can estimate that these studies represent close to five hundred hours of classroom observation. In 138 classes (including Flanders' experimental groups) 118 teachers had some type of systematic record made of their teaching behavior.

In the elementary school, reading and social studies classes were recorded by Hughes. Taba, who also worked in the elementary school, recorded only social studies classes. Additionally, Hughes reports a specimen record of observation for one "activity" period for each of twenty-five teachers in her sample. In the case of three teachers for whom no "activity" period was recorded, there is a specimen record in music for one, in writing for another, and in spelling for the third.

Of all the researchers, Flanders is the only one who concentrated his research wholly at the junior high school level, where he has recorded teacher-pupil interaction among seventh and eighth graders. Bellack and Smith have studied high school classes. Bellack has studied tenth and twelfth grade classes in a unit on economics in a Problems of Democracy class. Smith has studied ninth, tenth, eleventh, and twelfth grade classroom behavior in English, mathematics, science, history, and social studies classes. Therefore, except for Hughes, who has two kindergarten classes in her study, and thus six kindergarten observation records, twenty-five observations of "activity" lessons, and one observation each of a class in music, spelling, and writing, the major emphasis of all the other four research studies

TABLE I
Participants in All Studies Combined

Study	Number of Teachers	Number of Students	Number of Classes	Grade Level	Subjects	Number of Records Per Class	Time Taken
Bellack	15	345	15	10th	Problems of Democracy	4 regular h.s. periods	4 consecutive days
Flanders, Pilot Experimental	2	1,040	13 groups (20 each)	12th	560 students geometry	1 record of 2 hrs.,	one session on one day
Flanders, Major	32[a]	920	32[a]	8th	480 social studies	10 min. each	During 2 wk. unit, esp.
				8th-math. 7th-s.s.	481 math. 439 social studies	6 hrs. math. 10-12 social studies	beg. and end
Hughes, Pilot	6	ng[b]	6	1-1st 1-3rd 1-4th 1-5th 2-6th		4-30 min. records	Once each week for a month
Hughes, Major	35	ng[b]	35	Kdg-6	Kdg. reading activity –social studies	3-30 min. records	3 times within a 2½ month period
Taba	20	481	20	3-2nd gr. 5-3rd gr. 3-4th gr. 5-5th gr. 4-6th gr.	Social Studies	Four 1-hr. classes approx.	Four different times throughout school year
Smith	17	ng[b]	17[c]	5-9th gr. 3-10th gr. 5-11th gr. 4-12th gr.	Eng., math., science history (social st.)	5 per class	5 consecutive class periods

[a]One class in the Flanders' study had to be dropped.
[b]Not given.
[c]Tapes of three of seventeen not usable.

is in the academic areas. Smith, in speaking of his own work, has
said:

> Teachers also have all sorts of physical equipment to illustrate
> scientific principles, or to engage students in the task of thinking
> through scientific problems, but this aspect of teaching is left out of
> our account. Nevertheless, it is believed that the concepts suggested
> above will enable us to deal with most of the behavior manifested in the
> teaching of the so-called content subjects—mathematics, social studies,
> English, and science.[1]

Before beginning a description of the teachers who comprise the
subjects of these five studies, it is necessary to note that the aspect of
curriculum and teaching investigated by these studies often derive
from the major objectives of the study. Thus, Flanders, in discussing
the selection of teachers for his major study, writes:

> The teachers were not the sole object of our sampling; it was the
> teacher plus the students, the total classroom situation.
> The major purpose of sampling was to select about sixteen teacher-
> class units in which there would be a wide range of teacher influence
> yet the average characteristics of the entire sample would be generally
> representative of the two school systems. These conditions can be met
> by selecting classes that are equally extreme on some scale that is
> correlated with teacher influence.[2]

Similarly, since the central objective of Taba's study was the examination of the development of thought under optimum training conditions, her selection of teachers was also, like Flanders, influenced by
her major objective:

> Since training of teachers was involved and since, furthermore, the
> time available for the training was brief, it was important to select
> teachers with maximum motivation, a reasonable flexibility and a
> capacity to learn to change their teaching style.[3]

Since the sampling is generally of academic subjects in these five
studies, it follows that these studies have recorded no classes of the
special teacher, neither special in the sense of teaching a special
area—art, music, or shop—nor special in the sense of teacher of
special or exceptional children—gifted, retarded, physically or
mentally handicapped. Indeed, in the Flanders study, in which the
sample was drawn somewhat at random, a "special" class was included in the sampling and subsequently dropped.

---

[1] B. Othanel Smith, "Toward a Theory of Teaching," in Arno A. Bellack,
ed., *Theory and Research in Teaching* (New York: Bureau of Publications,
Teachers College, Columbia University, 1963), p. 3.
[2] Ned A. Flanders, "Teacher Influence, Pupil Attitudes, and Achievement:
Studies in Interaction Analysis," U.S. Office of Education, Cooperative Research
Project, No. 397 (Minneapolis: University of Minnesota, 1960), p. 41.
[3] Hilda Taba and others, "Thinking in Elementary School Children" (San
Francisco: San Francisco State College, 1964), p. 70.

Later on in our analysis we discovered that the class taught by teacher N702 was an abnormal class. It contained six sight-saving students whose visual disability was so great that they had to have all of our tests read by some other person. In addition, five students were assigned to this class because of emotional difficulties. For these reasons the class was dropped from the study.[4]

Although the teachers in the study do not represent teachers who are in any of the above-mentioned senses "special," there is evidence that they were not average or representative of teachers in general.

Bellack gives no information as to how his teachers were selected, and a random sample is nowhere suggested. Flanders, as already indicated, wanted the entire sample of his study to represent the two school systems from which they were drawn, but he arrived at this general representation by selecting classes equally extreme on a scale that ranged the children's perceptions of their teachers' influence. Thus, in choosing the teachers perceived by children as being most direct and most indirect, there can be no doubt that the individual teacher in Flanders' study is neither representative nor average. Additionally, of the hundred teachers who composed the universe from which Flanders wished to draw his sample, twenty-five would not agree to participate; this, too, affected randomization. In the Hughes study there were forty-one teachers, of whom thirty-one had been judged good by a supervisor. Of the other ten teachers in the study, Hughes writes:

Another group included in the major study were ten teachers from one school selected as representative of the twenty-five professional employees in the school. The district personnel nominated two from each grade. In some cases the district personnel saw one teacher in a given grade as "good" within the school and the other as one whose work was of such quality as to cause genuine concern. For some teachers no distinction could be made among the teachers.[5]

The process of selection of teachers for Smith's study was different from the other researchers. In fact, all of the researchers demonstrate a completely unique selection process. Smith selected five schools first, and then asked that teachers be "nominated" for the study from each of the five schools. Smith reports that the following details were sent to the schools in asking for their teacher "nominations":

1. Each teacher should be selected from one of the four subject fields of English, mathematics, science, and social studies.

[4] Ned A. Flanders, "Teacher Influence, Pupil Attitudes, and Achievement," p. 51.
[5] Marie M. Hughes and Associates, "The Assessment of the Quality of Teaching: A Research Report," U.S. Office of Education Cooperative Research Project No. 353 (Salt Lake City: University of Utah, 1959), p. 19.

2. Select the teachers on the basis of your own judgment of their competence as teachers. Teacher participation in this project would be voluntary, of course. Three out of the four teachers you select should be, in your judgment, teachers of high ability—in other words, from among the best teachers on your staff. The fourth teacher selected should be one of average competence in your judgment. If you object to selecting an average teacher, the fourth teacher may also be one of high ability.[6]

Thus, Smith's teacher group, like Hughes', had a high proportion, at least 75 per cent, of teachers judged good by a supervisor or administrator.

Taba's teacher selection process was, in large part, determined by the study. In addition to having to fulfill the requirement of "*maximum motivation, a reasonable flexibility, and a capacity to learn to change their teaching style,*" these teachers were nonrepresentative of teachers in general in another way. Taba writes: "Seven of the twenty teachers had been involved in the development of the field trial of the curriculum outlines they were using."[7]

Of all five studies, Bellack's is the only one that codes the subject content systematically. The ability to code the content systematically and reliably may derive from the design of the project, which held the content constant by specifying the material to be taught. It is therefore a matter for speculation as to whether, in future research, content that was not held constant could be similarly systematically and reliably coded.

In these five studies, what is reported is the researchers' perceptions of what is happening in the classroom, as indicated generally by the verbal behavior of teachers and students. It is not to be supposed that the perceptions of teachers, pupils, supervisors, and administrators are the same as the researchers'. Thus, while the views and sometimes the judgments of the researchers are reported, these studies generally give no information as to how others would interpret this same classroom verbal behavior.

Although generally this problem of possible difference in perception has not been dealt with in these studies, some of the studies report some information on this problem. The most ingenious attempt to deal with one aspect of differential perspective was devised by Carin in a study that was undertaken in conjunction with the Hughes project. In the Carin study, "Children's Perceptions of Selected Teaching Acts," a test was devised to measure student reac-

[6] B. Othanel Smith and Milton O. Meux, " A Study of the Logic of Teaching" (Urbana: Bureau of Educational Research, College of Education, University of Illinois, 1963), p. 201.

[7] Hilda Taba and others, "Thinking in Elementary School Children," p. 70.

tions to actual specimen records from the Hughes study which had already been coded by the researchers. Carin, in reporting his results, writes as follows:

> The investigator was impressed with the magnitude and intensity of the children's expressions of guilt, responsibility, inadequacy, and hostility; these expressions of feelings toward the self, the teacher, and the situations, were even more impressive when the story situations that elicited these feelings were analyzed.
>
> Most of the situations presented in the *School Situation Perception Test* would be considered as common, everyday occurrences, and yet strong feelings against the self developed in the children's responses to these situations. Furthermore, five out of the eight coded teaching acts (#4 Solicitous, #5 Encourage, #7 Do Something For, #9 Inform, #10 Checking Involvement) received many responses indicating negative feelings even though they were coded as teaching acts especially designed to benefit or enhance the individual.[8]

Bellack, in attempting to measure emotional tone in the classroom, abandoned his original plan to code emotional tone in the same time units in which verbal behavior was coded. Instead, students similar to those in the study responded to five-minute segments of the taped discourse and rated the emotional tone in terms of four dimensions of meaning: valence, activity, potency, and stability, derived from the semantic differential scale. While this information indicates students' perceptions of the teachers' tone, since the research staff did not code this material, no basis for judging the congruency between researchers and students exists.

Flanders' study presents a slightly different approach to this question of differential perception. The student's perception of the teachers as either direct or indirect was the basis for his entire teacher selection process:

> The Minnesota Student Attitude Inventory is an attitude test which has shown a significant correlation in earlier studies with the teacher's pattern of influence. For the present study a shortened form of the test was used. The test is made up of items that reflect the students' attitudes toward the teacher, the class activities, the teacher's system of rewards and punishments, and their dependence on the teacher.[9]

Thus, Flanders' study may be seen as set from the beginning within the students' perceptual framework. However, in evaluating the hypothesis, it is the researcher's perspective, and not the students', that is used. The significance of this shift will be discussed at length later.

[8] Arthur Carin, "Children's Perception of Selected Teaching Acts" (Unpublished doctoral dissertation, University of Utah, 1959), p. 273.

[9] Ned A. Flanders, "Teacher Influence, Pupil Attitudes, and Achievement," p. 41.

In addition to the areas already enumerated, Jackson indicates many other areas and facts of the teaching enterprise that still remain to be explored: "Another aspect of teaching that deserves more attention than it has received to date concerns the changes that take place in a classroom over a period of time."[10] Of the five studies, Taba's study is the one with the longest time duration, since her design consisted of four classroom observations for each class, spaced throughout one school year. Nevertheless, as Jackson indicates, the need for studies that trace longer developmental sequences is clear. The need for developmental studies may be of most pressing importance in studies that attempt to identify the outcome variables of such aspects as Hughes' "teacher power," Flanders' "direct and indirect influence," and Taba's "training of thinking."

A study of teacher behavior over time may be of equal, if not more crucial, importance. Many of the assumptions of teacher power and influence suggest that the teachers' influence and power is constant over time, and that it is the teachers' attitudes which influence the class, and not the class which influences the teachers:

> The rule is that when either type of contact predominates, domination incites further domination, and integration stimulates further integration. It is the teacher's tendency that spreads among pupils and is continued even when the teacher is no longer in the room. Furthermore, the pattern a teacher develops in one year is likely to persist in his classroom the following year with different pupils.[11]

Bellack's findings of great stability of teachers' verbal behavior might be considered confirmation of Flanders' assumption: "And notwithstanding occasional deviations these classroom patterns of discourse remain relatively stable over time."[12] However, Bellack's observations of teachers' verbal statements were made in a period of a week and in relation to the same classroom of students, and this may not be a sufficiently reliable test of teacher verbal stability over time. Evidence does exist to suggest that teacher verbal behavior is not stable over time; this evidence, which is in direct contradiction to Flanders' and Bellack's studies, is reported by Mitzel and Rabinowitz: "In non-statistical language the variation among teachers on different visits is of such magnitude that the variability among either teachers or visits is not made apparent for the majority of the statement categories."[13]

---

[10] Phillip Jackson, "The Way Teaching Is," *National Education Association Journal*, 54:13, November, 1965.

[11] Ned A. Flanders, "Teacher Influence, Pupil Attitudes and Achievement." p. 7.

[12] Arno A. Bellack et al., *The Language of the Classroom*, p. 63.

[13] Harold E. Mitzel and W. Rabinowitz, *Assessing Social-Emotional Climate in the Classroom by Withall's Technique*, Psychological Monographs, No. 368, 1953, p. 17.

Issues such as the effect of different class composition on teachers' behavior, the effects of experience, age, and other factors are now dealt with by either assuming or hypothesizing answers. Only longitudinal studies of teacher behavior will help illuminate the above-stated issues, which are all aspects of the question of teachers' stability over time.

Jackson suggests other areas of curriculum and teaching that need investigation:

> Furthermore, when we arrive, we typically keep our eyes closed or our tape recorder unplugged until the students have settled themselves down to business and the teacher stands up in front of the room with chalk in hand. All the preliminaries are merely background noise, we tell ourselves. But are they? The typical observer's sampling bias makes sense, but does so at the expense of ignoring the psychological reality of the classroom.[14]

Jackson speaks of the need to sample the first day of school because of its uniqueness:

> The first day of school, as an instance, is different from all others. It is then that initial impressions are formed and the foundations of enduring attitudes established. During those first few hours in the classroom, students are trying to decide whether their new teacher will be as good or as bad as the last; the teachers are trying to decide whether this will be an easy or a difficult class to handle.[15]

Bruno Bettelheim, in discussing a child's first day at a school for severely disturbed children, also speaks of the uniqueness of the first day. Bettelheim, of course, is speaking of the emotionally handicapped child's approach to a much more fearful situation, but Bettelheim, just as Jackson, recognizes the crucial nature of the first impact:

> Of all days at the school, the first is the most important for the child in forming an opinion of us and the school and for us in beginning those relations to him which may later become steppingstones toward solving his problems. Never again will he be as anxious about the school and as little prepared to admit it. Never again will he be as hopeful or fearful about his life there, about the adults and the other children, about the activities, and about how he will stack up in the new order. But never again will he be quite apt to misinterpret what he experiences, to distrust and to fight so clearly what he is most frightened about . . . .[16]

In addition to the suggestions Jackson makes for longitudinal studies, for studies of before-class activities, and for sampling the first day of school behavior, he makes some interesting comments about the public, semiprivate, and private dimensions of teaching:

[14] Phillip Jackson, "The Way Teaching Is," p. 13.
[15] *Ibid.*
[16] Bruno Bettelheim, *Love Is Not Enough* (Glencoe, Illinois: The Free Press, 1950), p. 38.

Little is known about the differences among these three instructional modes—public, semiprivate, and private—although common sense would seem to tell us that the educational environment created by each might differ in important ways from those created by the other two. To give an obvious example: When a teacher is alone with a student, he is not faced with the problems of control and management that frequently absorb a large portion of his energies in a group setting . . . .

. . . My impression is that teachers also laugh and smile more frequently when working individually with students. There is, then, a much greater sense of physical and psychological intimacy between teacher and student during these sessions than when the teacher is responding to the class as a group. [17]

Some interest in describing emotional tone and nonverbal behavior is evinced in several of these studies. Bellack's attempts to measure and judge emotional tone have already been described. Because Flanders' study uses a system in which observers make judgments while in the classroom, Flanders suggests that these observations should be based on the observer's response to the teacher's total effect. Thus, the observation would, of necessity, include emotional tone and bodily stance. Flanders writes:

Second, the trained observer is in the best position to judge whether the teacher is, in general, restricting or expanding the freedom of action of the student; if he feels that the pattern at the moment is restrictive, he is cautious in the use of the indirect categories; if he feels that the pattern at the moment expands freedom, he is cautious in the use of direct categories; but he remains alert to the total social situation.

At first, this ground rule seems to be an invitation to biased observation, yet there is a theory of the "unbiased, biased observer." The observer is biased in the sense that his categorization must be consistent with his general assessment of the teacher's intent for a given sequence of action. He is unbiased in that he remains open to all evidence that the general intent of the teacher may be changing.[18]

Hughes, who used a system of observation that entailed the stenographic recording of portions of classroom behavior called specimen records, instructed her observers: "You are to focus your attention upon the teacher and what he says and does. To the extent possible, record his non-verbal behavior."[19]

Although he does not specifically deal with emotional impact, Smith comments on the difficulty of securing evidence on the non-

[17] Phillip Jackson, "The Way Teaching Is," p. 12.

[18] Ned A. Flanders, "Teacher Influence, Pupil Attitudes, and Achievement," p. 7.

[19] Marie M. Hughes and Associates, "The Assessment of the Quality of Teaching," p. 38.

verbal aspects of classroom behavior when the coding of behavior is done from tape recordings. His comments are equally pertinent to studies such as Bellack's and Taba's:

> An important problem was to secure a record of as much as possible of what occurs in the classroom. Tape recordings can reproduce only the sounds of the classroom. But often a facial expression, a gesture, pointing, or nodding is essential to understanding the speaker exactly. We had no facilities for making a record of facial expressions and nods. However, we were able to make a record of gestures and points in some cases. In addition, a record was made of the physical contents and arrangements of the classroom, the size of the class, the materials used, etc. Finally, we found it advisable to note the causes of extraverbal sounds such as footsteps and machines. All of these things were noted so that we might refer to these sources while making subsequent analyses of the classroom discourse.
>
> To record these non-aural aspects a member of the project staff was seated in the back of the room with the machine operator. This observer secured the bibliographic data on all books used in class, the assignments given, and all materials used by students in preparing their reports as well as all dittoed material used in classroom discussion.[20]

Taba has only this to say about the inability to detect emotional tone within the design of her study: "It was assumed that by coding 'agreement' and 'disagreement' it would be possible to get some idea about the emotional tone employed by the teacher. Actually the agreement and the disagreement seem to have affected more the content of thought than the emotional climate."[21]

Generally, then, these five studies have not been primarily interested in charting or describing emotional or nonverbal behavior, nor have their results in this area been fruitful. Rather, they have concentrated on verbal behavior in the classrooms investigated, and not all aspects of verbal behavior either. For, as Flanders aptly points out, in speaking of his own work, all aspects of verbal behavior have not as yet been amenable to the kind of categorizing utilized in these studies:

> The system of categories is designed for situations in which the teacher and the students are actively discussing school work. It is an inappropriate tool when the verbal behavior is discontinuous, separated by fairly long periods of silence, when one person is engaged in prolonged lecturing, or is reading aloud to the class. In situations in which two-way communication does not exist and is not likely to exist, the observer should stop, make a note of the exact time at which spontane-

[20] B. Othanel Smith and Milton O. Meux, "A Study of the Logic of Teaching," p. 208.
[21] Hilda Taba and others, "Thinking in Elementary School Children," p. 146.

ous interaction lapsed and the reasons for the interruption. The observer must remain alert to the resumption of spontaneous interaction.[22]

In Smith's study, tapes of two mathematics classes could not be used because the amount of seat work done in the classes rendered the interpretation of the tapes unintelligible. Smith calls a monologue what Flanders identifies as *one person engaged in prolonged lecturing*. Smith, like Flanders, in his study, is interested not in the monologue but in the episode, a verbal transaction between two or more speakers. Bellack's coding system is the only one at present capable of dealing with monologue speech effectively, but the system cannot, like the others, deal with seat work, or what Jackson calls semiprivate and private teacher-pupil verbal interaction.

Thus, for many reasons, it is the public verbal speech of the classroom that these five studies investigated. Bellack gives the following reason:

> Indeed observation of what goes on in elementary and secondary schools reveals that classroom activities are carried on in large part in verbal interaction between students and teachers. The purpose of the research presented here is to study the teaching process through analysis of the linguistic behavior of teachers and students in the classroom. We focused on language as the main instrument of communication in teaching.[23]

While Bellack chose to investigate verbal classroom behavior because he views it as the main instrument for communication of language, Flanders suggests a slightly different reason for sampling verbal behavior:

> Interaction analysis is concerned primarily with verbal behavior. This can be observed with higher reliability than most non-verbal behavior. The assumption is made that the verbal behavior of an individual is an adequate sample of his total behavior. In the classroom we must assume that the verbal statements of a teacher are consistent with his non-verbal gestures, in fact, his total behavior. This assumption cannot easily be tested since it would take too long a period to develop reliable measures of non-verbal behavior.[24]

Flanders' and Bellack's statements will be discussed more fully in the next section, which deals with the assumptions made by each of these five studies.

[22] Ned A. Flanders, "Teacher Influence, Pupil Attitudes, and Achievement," Appendix F, p. 4.

[23] Arno A. Bellack et al., *The Language of the Classroom*, p. 1.

[24] Ned A. Flanders, "Teacher Influence, Pupil Attitudes, and Achievement," Appendix F, p. 2.

VIII

Assumptions of Each Study

It is clear that an assumption may be recognized before it can be challenged, and this fact indicates the importance to scientific progress of formulating explicitly all relevant assumptions in any hypothesis, allowing none of them to remain hidden.[1]

Several assumptions are common to all five studies, other assumptions are common to some of the studies and not to others, and some assumptions are unique to each study. Some of these general and specific assumptions have been alluded to earlier, but will be restated here so that the discussion may be as complete as possible. However, these assumptions, which are implicit in the observation and category systems of these studies, will be examined in those sections of this report that deal with the collection and analysis of information.

That aspects of the classroom enterprise exhibit observable regularities and can, therefore, be systematically and reliably identified, categorized, and tabulated is the assumption that is central to all research in curriculum and teaching, and these five studies are no exception. That the verbal behavior of the classroom is either one central aspect of classroom behavior that warrants investigation, as Bellack suggests, or that verbal behavior is a reliable measure of total behavior, as Flanders suggests, are two alternative assumptions of these studies.

Before continuing to recount other assumptions held in common by this group, it may be helpful to remark upon the assumptions concerning verbal behavior. What is generally coded in these studies is the researchers' perceptions of the data of observation. As demonstrated in the Carin study, all children do not always share the perceptions of the researchers. It should be noted further that, in the Carin study, children's perceptions of coded categories were checked against the Hughes study. In the Hughes study the researchers' per-

[1] Irving M. Copi, *Introduction to Logic*, 2nd ed. (New York: The Macmillan Company, 1961), p. 425.

ceptions were formed in the classrooms themselves and recorded stenographically with as many nonverbal acts as could possibly be detected. This being the case, it seems not unreasonable to suggest that in those studies—Bellack's, Smith's, and Taba's—in which codings were made on the basis of tape recordings, the researchers received far fewer cues to the total meaning of the speech act, and therefore were even further from the perspective of the students in the classroom than were the researchers in the Hughes study. For the untrained, the voice alone, when recorded, does not suggest the same total speech act as does the presence of a speaking person. To communicate by recorded voice alone the totality of the speech act is the job of a professional actor. This fact may account for the great difficulty of the Bellack study reliably to measure emotional tone in any manner except a gross classification.

Galloway asserts in his study that persons judge the intent of communication through an estimate of the communicant's nonverbal cues. The receiver of communication, says Galloway, believes that a person's nonverbal cues are a more reliable indication of the sender's state because they are believed to be less governable.

> During social interaction, the expressive acts of an individual's activity suggest a promissory character that is assumed by others to represent an accurate reflection of the real self an individual possesses. Moreover, expressive maneuvers enable others to perceive accurately the kind of individual being dealt with. Thus, an observer will gauge the accuracy of an individual's communication by the so-called ungovernable aspects of his expressive behavior as a check on the verbal which is considered more governable. In short, an observer will check upon the validity of the self that is being communicated by attending to the unconscious, unintended non-verbal behaviors of the actor.[2]

The issue, as just raised, is not intended to suggest that tape recordings are an inappropriate device for gathering information about classroom behavior, but rather to underscore the abstracting nature of tape recordings. The abstracting nature of tape recordings makes them not less valuable, but certain judgments based on tape recordings, especially judgments of emotional tone and intent, must be made with caution. A discussion of the various methods of observation and coding and the problems each present and solve will be discussed in a later section.

Aschner identifies a third assumption common to all five studies, with one possible exception, an assumption that often goes unrecognized and thus unanalyzed:

[2] Charles M. Galloway, "An Exploratory Study of Observational Procedures for Determining Teacher Non-verbal Communication" (Unpublished Doctoral Project Report, University of Florida, Gainesville, June, 1962), p. 32.

The commonly held assumption that each person is responsible and accountable for his acts is clearly reflected in the behaviors of teachers and students in the classroom. Despite all their college courses in psychology, teachers seem not to see themselves as manipulators of student behavior by push-button techniques. Nor does anyone appear to view the student as emitting verbal responses conditioned to follow upon given environmental stimuli. If a student makes a mistaken or an impertinent reply to a teacher's question he is normally corrected or called to account. Now if this student's reply were looked upon as mere conditioned response, it would be plainly absurd to hold him accountable for it. (After all, Pavlov's dogs cannot be blamed for slavering when the bell rings.) Rather the teacher would be obliged simply to conclude that he had pushed the wrong buttons. But of course this is just not the way people see themselves or others, in or out of school. The definition of verbal behavior proposed herein is frankly acknowledged to reflect the accustomed ways in which people deal with one another in group discussion situations and descriptions of verbal interaction, based on a definition assuming a view of human action consonant with that upon which the subjects of observation themselves proceed, should be useful to those who hope ultimately to bring about desired change in teaching.[3]

Flanders, in agreeing with Aschner's position, not only sees the teacher as responsible for his verbal behavior, but also goes further in viewing the teacher as capable of modifying his verbal patterns:

... an assumption necessary to the application of these research results in any program designed to increase teacher effectiveness is that teachers can control their verbal participation in the classroom.[4]

It is interesting to speculate on whether Aschner's assumption that persons are responsible for their verbal behavior in classroom discourse, rather than agents whose responses are conditioned by environmental stimuli, will remain an implicit assumption in studies of classroom discourse if evidence of great classroom verbal regularity continues to accumulate. What may now stand as a generally agreed upon hypothesis might be more critically examined if the suggested systematic nature of classroom behavior proposed by Bellack is substantiated by further research.

It was suggested earlier that one study—that of Bellack—does not share the Aschner assumption *that each person is responsible and accountable for his acts.* Indeed, Bellack comes close to suggesting an entirely different position. For example, the following is a descrip-

[3] Mary Jane Aschner, "The Language of Teaching," *Teachers College Record*, 61:251, February, 1960.
[4] Ned A. Flanders, "Teacher Influence, Pupil Attitudes, and Achievement: Studies in Interaction Analysis," U.S. Office of Education Cooperative Research Project No. 397 (Minneapolis: University of Minnesota, 1960), p. 112.

tion of the *responding move*, one of Bellack's four pedagogical moves:

> *Responding*—These moves bear a reciprocal relationship to soliciting moves and occur only in relation to them. Their pedagogical function is to fulfill the expectation of soliciting moves. Thus, students' answers to teachers' questions are classified as responding moves.[5]

The use of the classroom game metaphor, coupled with definitions such as the one quoted above, indicates that the classroom enterprise, as seen in the Bellack study, has aspects that occur irrespective of the persons involved. It is the functioning of the enterprise itself which calls forth a certain kind of response, rather than the persons involved. This analysis might be seen as being system-oriented rather than person-oriented.

Cogan, like Aschner, identifies another assumption that often goes unrecognized, and yet is incorporated into these studies: "The chain of interaction between teacher and pupil is arbitrarily considered to start with the behavior of teachers."[6]

Cogan's comment on the arbitrary nature of beginning the study of classroom interaction with the behavior of the teacher suggests the possibility of viewing many of the concepts presented by these five studies from a slightly different perspective. Indeed, if the Cogan position is linked to the position that Aschner presents but does not support—that is, that there may be conditions in the classroom that call forth certain responses—even greater interpretive possibilities suggest themselves.

All these studies, with the possible exception of the Bellack study, assume that the teacher is the agent in control of the classroom situation. Hughes and Flanders make this notion of teacher control or influence their central concept. By so doing, they take the position that mitigation of this control is a positive value. Smith sees the teacher as the agent in potential control of the logical processes of the students who could, if he wished, release pupil creativity and develop pupil initiative. Taba holds the teachers responsible for the development of student thinking. Bellack, who is furthest from this position, nevertheless views the teacher as the least restricted, most free person in the classroom. Yet Bellack does mention an aspect of the teaching enterprise that makes the teacher dependent upon the student:

> In gauging wins and losses, players should keep in mind that this is not a game in which one player, such as the teacher, wins while another

---

[5] Arno A. Bellack et al., *The Language of the Classroom*, p. 4.

[6] M. L. Cogan, "Theory and Design of a Study of Teacher-Pupil Interaction," *The Harvard Educational Review*, 26:325, 1956.

player, such as one of the pupils, loses. Rather, there are relative degrees of winning and losing, and the teacher's winnings are a function of the pupils' performances. This is a peculiar, but important, characteristic of this game. While the teacher undeniably has the greater power and freedom in the course of play, he is ultimately dependent on his pupils for the degree of success he achieves in playing the game.[7]

To reverse the commonly held assumption that the teacher is the power figure in the classroom, and think of the teacher as the limited and controlled agent in the classroom situation suggests entirely new ideas:

> Our progress in genuine knowledge always consists in part in the discovery of something not understood in what had previously been taken for granted as plain, obvious, matter-of-course and in part in using meanings that are directly grasped as instruments for getting hold of obscure and doubtful meanings.[8]

Recall that in Smith's definition of teaching, he suggests that there are certain aspects of the classroom over which the teacher has no control: ". . . one set over which the agent has no control (e.g., size of classroom, and physical characteristics of pupils)."[9]

Wayland, in "The Teacher as Decision-Maker," claims that the limitations on the teacher are very great indeed. Wayland speaks of the teacher as a functionary in an essentially bureaucratic system:

> . . . As such, he is a replaceable unit in a rationally organized system, and most of the significant aspects of work are determined for him. Any areas in which he makes decisions are those which are given to him and are not inherent in his role as teacher. They may therefore be altered, increased or removed completely.[10]

After Wayland enumerates nine reasons for the great limitations on teachers' behavior: need for integration, division of labor, rationalization of the work, differences in personality and technical competence of the staff, the limitation of time, traditions of the local school, public responsibility of the chief administrator, turnover in staff, and the large size of school systems, he states:

> These nine factors, operating within most school systems, set the limits on the decision-making of the teacher within the system. As a functionary in that system *whom he will teach; where, when, and for*

---

[7] Arno A. Bellack et al., *The Language of the Classroom*, p. 239.

[8] John Dewey, *How We Think*, rev. ed. (Boston: D. C. Heath and Co., 1933), p. 140.

[9] B. Othanel Smith and Milton O. Meux, "A Study of the Logic of Teaching" (Urbana: Bureau of Educational Research, College of Education, University of Illinois, 1963), p. 3.

[10] Sloan Wayland, "The Teacher as Decision Maker," in A. Harry Passow, ed., *Curriculum Crossroads* (New York: Bureau of Publications, Teachers College, Columbia University, 1962), p. 43.

how long he will teach; how he will evaluate the work of the student; and (in a measure) how he will teach are determined for the teacher.[11]

The answers to questions of who is controlling whom in the classroom and just how varied classroom behavior is await further and more lengthy investigation. It is, however, of interest to note that while Flanders wrote that teachers' statements continuously shift from direct to indirect in a sequence of unending variety, Bellack, using a different category system and statistical analysis, was able to state:

> This refined ability to predict is probably best illustrated in terms of initiation of teaching cycles. By using data such as frequency and percentage distributions in combination with Markov matrices, one can describe not only the relative proportion of teacher-to-pupil initiated cycles, but the probabilities of certain linguistic events following certain other linguistic events. In terms of simple frequency for the group of fifteen teachers, teacher-initiated cycles far outnumber pupil-initiated cycles; but when the preceding state is a pupil-initiated cycle, another pupil-initiated cycle is almost as likely to occur as a teacher-initiated cycle. For one class of the fifteen, the probability of a pupil-initiated cycle occurring under these circumstances is even somewhat greater than for a teacher-initiated cycle. While it is not possible to generalize the present data to all kinds of teaching on all levels, the regularities in the patterning of classroom discourse in the present sample suggest the hypothesis that similar kinds of regularities may be found in other samples of classroom verbal behavior.[12]

The common position held by most of these studies—that the teacher is in active, thoughtful control of the teaching situation—has another corollary assumption that is also held in common by these studies. This corollary assumption is the implicitly or explicitly stated belief that the teachers' behavior in the classroom is determined, or should be determined, by his goals for the students. Flanders and Hughes instruct the teachers to use those verbal patterns that will mitigate their power components in the classroom. Smith's definition of teaching's essential features has previously been quoted as comprising an agent, a situation, and an *end-in-view*. Bellack, too, at times postulates a teacher who uses questions to affect certain kinds of pupil behavior, who has clearly defined intentions behind his questions, which the researcher can identify, and who expects certain kinds of responses from his students. For example:

> In the analysis of the soliciting move and of the responding move as separate moves, one is concerned with the intentional meaning of the soliciting move and with the intrinsic meaning of the responding move. In analyzing the intentional meaning of the solicitation, one asks,

[11] *Ibid.*, p. 48.
[12] Arno A. Bellack et al., *The Language of the Classroom*, p. 217.

"What action does the solicitor intend to elicit?" In analyzing the intrinsic meaning of the responding move, one asks, "What does the respondent say?"

In the analysis of the relationships of the soliciting move and the responding move in the soliciting-responding act, one is interested in the consequential meaning of the soliciting move and the relational meaning of the responding move: that is, in the relation between the intended response and actual response. In analyzing the consequential nature of the solicitation, one asks, "Does the soliciting move elicit the intended response?" In analyzing the relational meaning of the responding move, one asks, "How does what the respondent says relate to what the solicitor intended to elicit?" In this research, the analysis of the soliciting-responding act is in terms of the relational meaning of the response—that is, to what extent does the responding move reflect the intentional meaning of the soliciting move? [13]

Taba takes the strongest position possible on stressing the ability of the teacher to be in total control of verbal behavior in the classroom situation, and to use this control to further identifiable ends: "The fact was stressed that all learning experiences must serve identifiable functions, and that nothing should be happening in a classroom which a teacher could not justify in terms of objectives." [14]

Jackson calls into question the assumption that the teacher should be or even can be working within a framework of goal-oriented behavior while interacting with the class. He suggests that it is before class interaction begins that the teacher's behavior is characterized by careful planning and rational deliberation, but that this is not the teacher's behavior when "on the firing line":

Behavior relevant to the teaching task includes many things, such as preparing lesson plans, arranging furniture and equipment within the room, marking papers, studying test reports, reading sections of a textbook, and thinking about the aberrant behavior of a particular student. Indeed, these activities, most of which occur when the teacher is alone, are so crucial to the teacher's performance during the regular teaching sessions that they would seem to deserve the label "preactive" teaching. This designation commands our attention and helps us distinguish this class of behavior from the "interactive" teaching activities that occur *vis-à-vis* the students.

One of the chief differences between preactive and interactive teaching behavior seems to be in the quality of the intellectual activity involved. Preactive behavior is more or less deliberative. Teachers, when grading exams, planning a lesson, or deciding what to do about a particularly difficult student, tend to weigh evidence, to hypothesize about the possible outcome of certain action, and so forth. At such times, teaching looks like a highly rational process.

Contrast this with what happens when the students enter the room.

[13] *Ibid.*, p. 93.
[14] Hilda Taba and others, "Thinking in Elementary School Children" (San Francisco: San Francisco State College, 1964), p. 61.

In the interactive setting, the teacher's behavior is more or less spontaneous. When students are in front of him, the teacher tends to do what he feels or knows is right rather than what he reasons is right. This is not to say that thought is absent when class is in session, but it is thought of quite a different order.

There appear to be two major reasons for this shift. For one thing, by their questions, requests, and reactions, students, to some extent, control what the teacher does, and therefore much that goes on during a teaching session is predictable in only a general way. The specifics must be dealt with as they happen, and many of them do not call for prolonged and involved thought.

Another reason for the difference in cognitive style between preactive and interactive teaching has to do with the rapidity of events in the classroom. Research suggests that things happen rather quickly during a teaching session. For example, my own observations indicate that the elementary teacher may change the focus of his concern as many as 1,000 times daily. Amid all this hustle and bustle, the teacher often has little time to think. [15]

In considering the major assumptions that are unique to the Bellack study, issues raised by Bellack's treatment of language and meaning, task, and his use of the game metaphor will be explored. In Bellack's category system, as in all category systems, there are implicit and explicit assumptions, but these will be dealt with more economically when the category system is explored.

Bellack, at the beginning of his first report, states:

> We assumed that the primary function of language is the communication of meaning and that describing linguistic events in the classroom in terms of the meanings expressed by teachers and students was a potentially fruitful direction for research. Our concept of the nature of meaning was derived in large measure from Wittgenstein's view that "the meaning of a word is its use in the language." Equation of meaning and use suggested that the problem here was that of identifying the distinctive functions language actually serves in the verbal interplay between students and teachers and hence what meanings are conveyed through the words they use. [16]

The use of the phrase "conveyed meanings" in the Bellack study raises a difficulty that lies at the heart of content analysis. If a teacher asks a student to explain the uses of a protective tariff and the student does so, the observer has, it would seem, adequate grounds for judging that some kind of meaning has been communicated between student and teacher, and vice versa. Similarly, if a student offers an answer that the observer judges to be incongruent with the teacher's question, the observer has logical grounds for judging that a certain kind of meaning has not been communicated.

---

[15] Phillip Jackson, "The Way Teaching Is," *National Education Association Journal*, 54:11, November, 1965.

[16] Arno A. Bellack et al., *The Language of the Classroom*, p.. 2.

However, it is suggested here that the term "conveyed meanings" conveys more meaning than meaning in the sense of manifest vocabulary word meaning. In all discussions of the use of content analysis, although there is widespread agreement as to the observer's ability to observe and analyze manifest meaning, the ability to observe and analyze latent content always raises serious questions, for how much can be inferred from what is observed is a matter of opinion.

It is important to recall that the original intent of the project was to have the emotional tone and nuances of the language analyzed simultaneously with the words themselves. If this plan had been successful, perhaps one would be better able to speak of the "meanings conveyed" through the words teachers and students use. Even if one were reliably and consistently to code the emotional as well as the cognitive effect of word patterns, it would still be possible to ask if one has identified the meaning that teachers and students convey through the words they use. Presumably when Bellack speaks of meanings teachers and students convey, he is speaking of the meanings they convey to each other, and not to the researcher. Therefore, until we know what meanings are being delivered to the students by the teachers' words, in addition to the manifest substantive or instructional ones, it is questionable to speak of "conveyed meanings" at all. One teacher, in setting an instructional task, may say "Your homework must be in tomorrow!" Whether this statement is taken as a command that must be obeyed or a mild suggestion that a student can disregard with impunity might depend, in addition to the words used, on the momentary emotional tone it conveys, on the teacher's reputation, history of dealings with the class, his forms of reward and punishments, the motivation, fears, and anxieties of the students, and perhaps many other factors.

Bellack talks of a classroom or teaching "game" which includes a number of "sub-games." Bellack defines his sub-games as follows:

> Just as a football game consists of four quarters of play and a baseball game of nine innings, the classroom game is made up of segments which we designated "sub-games." In this research, the unit on international trade is viewed as a classroom game. Within this game, there are sub-units or sub-games, each of which is identified primarily by the type of activity that is the focus of attention during a given period of play. Student debates, class discussions, viewing films, pupil reports, and taking examinations are examples of activities of sub-games. [17]

The assertion that Bellack makes concerning the "game" of teaching, when explored fully, leads to the conclusion suggested earlier that

---

[17] *Ibid.*, p. 33.

the teaching enterprise has aspects that operate independently of the persons involved. The notion that there are implicit rules in teaching that guide the actions or moves of the participants may be seen as an interpretation of teaching in which the actions of the participants are guided by the forces of the system independent of the desires, abilities, will, and feelings of the teachers and students. This assumption clearly moves in an entirely different direction from the Aschner assumption concerning the nature of teacher and student classroom behavior. It was quoted earlier as: ". . . *The commonly held assumption that each person is responsible and accountable for his acts.*"

For contrast, let us look at Bellack's assertion:

> In playing the game, each player must follow a specific set of rules. If one plays the role of teacher in this game, he will follow one set of rules; if one plays the role of pupil, he will follow a somewhat different, though complementary, set of rules. One is permitted some deviations from these rules and the subsequent pattern will characterize one's individual style of play. These deviations, however, are infrequent and are relatively minor in comparison to the general style of expectations. In fact, the first rule, which might be called "the rule of rules," is that if one is to play the game at all, he will consistently follow the rules specified for his role. Otherwise, the game cannot be played. [18]

Bellack, in discussing his game metaphor, postulates a game in which teachers and students play a somewhat different, though complementary, set of rules. Bellack suggests that the game's final "payoff" is gauged by the amount of learning students are able to display after a set period of play.

If one examines Bellack's assertion that the teachers' ability to win the "teaching game" depends upon the pupils' performance, several problems become apparent. All the statements Bellack makes about the games are pure conjecture, since no evidence is offered in support of the claims about "classroom and/or teaching games"; indeed, the very design of the study precluded the possibility of gathering evidence to illuminate the issues. It is being suggested here that many of the statements made in this study about the "teaching game" might more helpfully be transplanted into problems for research investigation than left in the area of speculation and conjecture.

For example: Do teachers and pupils play the same game? Indeed, do all teachers play the game the same? How do teachers evaluate their teaching; is it in terms of pupil learnings? How do others evaluate teachers' classroom behavior? Are there many different ways of evaluating teachers? In *The Sociology of Teaching*, Wal-

[18] *Ibid.*, p. 237.

ler speaks speculatively of the persons who are important to the teacher:

> The significant people for a school teacher are other teachers and by comparison with good standing in that fraternity the good opinion of students is a small thing and of little price. A landmark in one's assimilation to the profession is that moment when he decides that only teachers are important. [19]

Thus, Waller suggests that the teacher rates himself or sees himself in relationship to other teachers, not in relationship to his students. Hopefully one can find some answers to these questions and speculations in the empirical realm. Researchers might find the concept of "classroom and teaching game" useful in gaining insight into these questions. It is less helpful to use this concept to obscure these questions.

In discussing some aspects of the assumptions of the Flanders study, it will be noted in which instances these assumptions are also exhibited in the Hughes study, which has a similar conceptual base. The particular attitudes toward freedom and authority that Flanders shares with Hughes have been discussed. Flanders speaks of his study as primarily concerned with the *spontaneous* interaction between teacher and student. As his study develops, Flanders indicates his belief in the teacher's ability to control his classroom verbal behavior when sufficiently well motivated. The dictionary definition of spontaneous is: "1. caused by natural impulse or desire; not forced or compelled; not planned beforehand; *a spontaneous cheer.* 2. taking place without external cause or help; caused entirely by inner forces. 3. growing or produced naturally; not planted, cultivated, etc."[20] The dictionary defines the verb "control" in the following manner: "1. have power or authority over; direct. 2. hold back; keep down; restrain. 3. regulate."[21] Since Flanders stipulated no special definition for these words in his study, it is to be expected that the common definition of spontaneous and control would be used in understanding Flanders' position. If this is the case, one must conclude that there is, at the very least, the suggestion of a contradiction when one asks teachers to control their verbal behavior in the spontaneous interaction of the classroom.

The suggestion has already been made that one might view the teacher as the person in the classroom who is the controlled and

[19] Willard Waller, *The Sociology of Teaching* (New York: John Wiley and Sons, 1932), p. 389.
[20] Clarence L. Barnhart, *Thorndike-Barnhart Comprehensive Desk Dictionary* (Garden City, N.Y.: Doubleday and Co., 1951), p. 746.
[21] Clarence L. Barnhart, *Thorndike-Barnhart Comprehensive Desk Dictionary.*

circumscribed one, as an alternative to the Flanders and Hughes position, which views the teacher as the major authority or influential figure in the classroom. In extending this concept further, two additional factors can be indicated. The role of the school in helping to socialize the young may account for the directness of teacher influence with young children. The school may be discharging one of the latent functions society expects of it. Conant clearly indicates this view of the elementary school teacher's function:

> The child enters the elementary school largely unsocialized, since he has had little prior opportunity to develop the simple habits on which the group activity depends. While the university teacher need only enforce the habits of restraint least partially built before, the elementary teacher starts almost from scratch, though of course the parents are engaged simultaneously in the same task. The maintenance of discipline among the very young is therefore quite a different problem from that faced by the college teachers and somewhat different from that of the secondary school teacher.[22]

The limiting effect of the group upon the teacher is not discussed in either the Flanders or the Hughes studies. It is assumed that it is the teacher who does the influencing, and although both Flanders and Hughes speak of classroom interaction, they do not indicate that this interaction can affect teacher behavior. Common sense tells us that the teacher does modify her behavior in terms of the age, experience, and background of her students. Sherif, in discussing the Lewin, Lippit, and White studies, from which Flanders and Hughes both draw much of their theoretical insights, discusses the group's effect upon the leader:

> The pioneering study of leadership by Lewin, Lippit, and White has been taken to mean that group processes are primarily or even wholly determined by the leadership techniques employed. Although this was not the concern of the study, it gives us some indication that the structure and traditions (norms) established in the group also exerted some influence. It is not possible to specify the exact nature of this influence, but had the investigators been concerned with this problem they would have certainly specified more fully the aggressive reactions of one group with an "autocratic" leader and the apathetic behavior of another in these terms—in assessing the weight of leadership determining the directions of the group, we have to consider seriously the structure of the group, including the power structure, its norms and major objectives which tend to set limits for the permissible latitude or range in which changes can be effected without bringing about various kinds of internal frictions. It will be well worth the effort if leadership study along interaction lines concentrates on the rest of the group as well as to determine under what conditions and by what means the group's

---

[22]James B. Conant, *The Education of American Teachers* (New York: McGraw-Hill Book Co., 1963), p. 116.

latitude of change can be increased to include within its limits a great number of alternatives.[23]

Flanders and Hughes both indicate negative attitudes toward teacher lecturing and the giving of information. Flanders categorizes lecturing or the giving of the teacher's own ideas as a direct influence, that is, one that restricts the freedom of action of a student by setting restraints or by focusing the student's attention on an idea. Similarly, Hughes codes as *imposition* the giving of information to the child when the information is not expressly requested. Flanders and Hughes both assume that students know best when they need information, and that the teacher functions best when he clarifies, encourages, stimulates, and acts as a resource person. Where students are to get their ideas is never identified, unless the implication of the Flanders and Hughes approach to education is that teaching involves bringing out of the students what is already there. Flanders and Hughes both conceive of the teacher who teaches least, in the sense of talking or "imposing" his own ideas and knowledge upon the class, as teaching best. Dewey deals with this issue to some extent in *How We Think*:

> The practical problem of the teacher is to preserve a balance between so little showing and telling as to fail to stimulate reflection and so much as to choke thought. Provided the student is genuinely engaged upon a topic, and provided the teacher is willing to give the student a good deal of leeway as to what he assimilates and retains (not requiring rigidly that everything be grasped or reproduced), there is comparatively little danger that one who is himself *enthusiastic will communicate too much* concerning a topic. If a genuine community spirit pervades the group, if the atmosphere is that of free communication in a developing exchange of experience and suggestions it is absurd to debar the teacher from the privilege and responsibility freely granted to the young, that of contributing his share. The only warning is that the teacher should not forestall the contributions of pupils, but should enter especially at the critical juncture where the experience of pupils is too limited to supply just the material needed.[24]
>
> In reality the teacher is the intellectual leader of a social group. He is a leader, not in virtue of official position but because of wider and deeper knowledge and matured experience.[25]

The concept of student dependency is very central to Flanders' study. Flanders places upon the teacher the obligation of changing students' response patterns from a dependent one to an independent one:

---

[23] M. Sherif and C. W. Sherif, *Groups in Harmony and Tension* (New York: Harper and Co., 1953), p. 48.

[24] John Dewey, *How We Think*, p. 270.

[25] *Ibid.*, p. 273.

One way to start discussing student reactions to teacher influence is to postulate that dependence is always present in some degree in any teacher-pupil relationship.

. . . One way to describe the process of instruction is to say that the teacher strives to change the response pattern of a student from merely complying to an authority figure to more independent actions that are determined by the student's own analysis of the subject matter problems confronting him. This is a shift from an authority orientation to a content-problem orientation.

. . . The first complication of this oversimplification is that students differ in their ability to give up their dependence on the teacher by shifting their orientation to the problem requirements. Some students cannot separate the problem requirements from teacher approval and continually seek teacher support at nearly all stages of their activities. We call such students *dependent prone*. Even the most skillful teachers find it difficult to stimulate self-directed problem solving among high dependent prone students. Dependence proneness is a personality trait that is established early in childhood and the extent to which it can be modified by school experiences is unknown.[26]

Flanders assumes dependency to be a negative characteristic although at one point he suggests that a certain *amount* of dependency is desirable. However, Flanders never explicates this statement but continues to urge the teacher to use her influence to control the level of dependence in the class.

Dewey looked at dependency from a different perspective and saw dependency as a positive power:

Taken absolutely, instead of comparatively, immaturity designates a positive force or ability—the power to grow. We do not have to draw out or educe positive activities from a child, as some educational doctrines would have it. Where there is life, there are already eager and impassioned activities. Growth is not something done to them—it is something they do. The positive and constructive aspect of possibility gives the key to understanding the two chief traits of immaturity, dependence and plasticity. It sounds absurd to hear dependence spoken of as something positive, still more absurd as a power. Yet if helplessness were all there were in dependence, no development could ever take place. A merely impotent being has to be carried, forever, by others. The fact that dependence is accompanied by growth in ability, not by an ever-increasing lapse into parasitism, suggests that it is already something constructive.

. . . From a social standpoint, dependence denotes a power rather than a weakness; it involves interdependence. There is always a danger that increased personal independence will decrease the social capacity of an individual. In making him more self-reliant, it may make him more self-sufficient; it may lead to aloofness and indifference. It often makes an individual so insensitive in his relations to others as to develop an illusion of being really able to stand and act alone—an unnamed

[26]Ned A. Flanders, "Teacher Influence, Pupil Attitudes, and Achievement," p. 13.

form of insanity which is responsible for a large part of the remediable suffering in the world.[27]

Before ending the discussion of the assumptions that Flanders alone and Flanders and Hughes both make, it is interesting to note the fact that Flanders urges teachers to use their influence to control the level of student dependence. Flanders then can be seen as suggesting that teacher influence and power may be put to good use. Thus it can be argued that the mitigation of teacher influence may not be the only responsible use of such influence. This suggests that if one asserts the position, as do Flanders and Hughes, that teachers have great power and influence in the classroom, one might postulate that this power and influence can be put to good use and the mitigation of power may not be the only responsible use of power.

Earlier in this study, a rather lengthy explication of Smith's assumptions on the benefits to be derived from a more logical approach to teaching was undertaken. This assumption and the assumptions implied in Smith's definition of teaching have already been rather fully amplified and thus will not be repeated. However, a brief discussion of one point made by Smith in discussing teaching may be of interest. When one compares Smith's statement on teaching:

> Teaching is assumed here to be a social phenomenon, fundamentally the same from one culture to another and from one time to another in the same culture. It has its own elements, forms, regularities, and problems. It takes place under what seems to be a relatively constant set of conditions—time limits, authority figures, student ability limits, institutional structures, etc.[28]

with that of Wayland's, two entirely opposite sets of assumptions about teaching are revealed: "One cannot meaningfully discuss *the* role of the teacher as if there were a timeless pattern of behavior appropriate for the teacher in any social setting. And it is unlikely that many would take such an extreme position."[29]

Of the five studies, the assumptions underlying the Taba study are the most difficult to identify, unravel, and discuss. This is largely so because Taba herself does not render her assumptions explicit and compounds one untested series of assumptions with another. Taba begins with the statement that her study's prime objective is to study the effect upon thinking of optimal training conditions. She speaks of using Piaget's work as a basis for her study. In what way the Piaget work functions within her study is not clearly explained; however, a

[27]John Dewey, *Democracy in Education* (New York: The Macmillan Co., 1961), p. 50.
[28]B. Othanel Smith and Milton O. Meux, "A Study of the Logic of Teaching," p. 2.
[29]Sloan Wayland, "The Teacher as Decision Maker," p. 42.

great deal of Piaget terminology is used, but in a sense that is entirely different from Piaget's. Piaget divides the development of thinking into three stages: the preoperational stage, from two to seven years of age, the concrete-operational stage, from seven to eleven years of age, and the formal-operational stage, from eleven years upward. Taba speaks of levels of thought in an entirely different way. Taba suggests that there is a hierarchical process within thinking itself, and that if this process is mastered, students can enter the Piaget-named formal-operational stage of thinking at an earlier age than Piaget suggests. With no evidence to support the notion, Taba takes three cognitive tasks—grouping and labeling, interpreting and making inferences, and predicting consequences—places them in a hierarchical order, suggests that the mastery of the "lower levels" precedes the mastery of the higher levels. She further states that the mastery of these steps makes possible the earlier emergence of formal thought in the Piaget sense. Now some types of grouping and labeling are extremely easy and some are extremely difficult. As Bruner indicates, in his *Study of Thinking*, disjunctive classification is very difficult for most adults. For example, while it is easy to understand a classification that includes all blondes but excludes all brunettes, it is not as easy to understand a classification system that includes all blondes, all former blondes, all brunettes who are planning to become blondes and thus excludes only those brunettes who were never blondes and who never intend to become blonde.

The assumption of a hierarchical order in the three cognitive tasks suggested by Taba is supported by no evidence on her part and none that could be found. To contend that predictive generalizations independent of their nature are more difficult than grouping and labeling independent of the task seems difficult to support:

> What of desks and tables, garages and barns, musical comedies and grand operas, Holsteins and Guernseys, schizophrenics and manic-depressives? It seems clear that most of our categorical furniture is cultural and that its presence in our minds is not guaranteed by the sensible attributes of the categories themselves. We need some sort of indication from those who participate in the culture of the things they treat as equivalents and those that are distinguished.
>
> Society as a whole recognizes that some terms involve semantic rules, rules whose appreciation requires a lifetime of study. The general population may bandy these terms about but when their application is important everyone else stands back to hear professional counsel.[30]

Most children can predict that if a ball is thrown up, it will fall down, and that if a glass is turned over, its contents will spill out, and

---

[30] Roger Brown, *Words and Things* (Glencoe, Ill.: The Free Press, 1958), p. 208.

if they put their hands in fire, they will be burned. Are these not predictive generalizations, and are they not more easily taught than the quite-simple grouping of trees into either a deciduous or conifer class? Another aspect of this issue has to do with the nature of grouping. Grouping and labeling are performed in terms of a concept; it is difficult to understand how, if this is so, one can think of grouping and labeling as leading upward toward generalization. To group cars, planes, automobiles, and trucks under the larger term of transportation, one needs to know the general term transportation first. How then can we logically speak of building up from grouping to a generalization, if grouping cannot take place independent of the generalization? Can we group round things together before the nature of the concept of roundness has been learned? Here it is suggested that the entire idea of grouping and labeling existing at a lower or separate order from generalizations has not been substantiated: "Opportunities for the active processing of information may provide the necessary conditions for the evolution and organization of abstract conceptual schemes. This preparation lays the groundwork for formal thinking, for manipulation of abstract concepts."[31]

Taba, in speaking of formal thinking, equates it with the manipulation of abstract concepts. Throughout her study, she suggests that when children manipulate abstract concepts below the age of eleven, they are indicating that formal thought is possible at an age younger than that suggested by Piaget. How different is this interpretation of the Piaget's stage of formal thought from that of Flavell's.

Flavell differentiates the stage of concrete operations from formal operations by stressing the concreteness of the younger child's orientation. It is not that the child cannot think in abstract terms, it is that he only goes beyond the concrete when he must. The adolescent, on the other hand, begins the solving of a problem by moving away from the concrete. Thus a child's ability to manipulate an abstract concept does not, as Taba suggests, indicate that formal thought is possible at an age below that which Piaget suggests. For it is in the differing manner with which the child and adolescent approaches problems that we distinguish the later stage from the earlier one.

> But the starting point for the concrete operations as for preoperations is always real rather than the potential. The child of seven to eleven years acts as though his primary task were to organize and order what is immediately present; the limited extrapolation of this organization and ordering to the not there is something he will do where necessary but this extrapolation is seen as a special-case activity. What he

[31] Hilda Taba and others, "Thinking in Elementary School Children," p. 22.

does not do (and what the adolescent does do) is delineate all possible eventualities at the outset and then try to discover which of these possibilities really do occur in the present data; in this latter strategy, the real becomes a special case of the possible; not the other way around. [32]

The most important general property of formal-operational thought, the one from which Piaget derives all others concerns the *real* versus the *possible.*

Unlike the concrete-operational child, the adolescent begins his consideration of the problem at hand by trying to envisage all the possible relations which could hold true in the data and then attempts, through a combination of experimentation and logical analysis, to find out which of these possible relations in fact do hold true. Reality is thus conceived as a special subset within the totality of things which the data would admit as hypotheses; it is seen as the "is" portion of a "might be" totality, the portion it is the subject's job to discover. [33]

The children in the Taba sample range in age from six years, eight months to twelve years, nine months, the mean age being nine years, five months. Although most of the children in the Taba sample would be at the age that Piaget designates as concrete-operational, some older children would already have entered the stage Piaget defines as formal thought, and some of the younger children would be in the preoperational stage. This wide age range raises two additional points. First, some of the evidence that Taba offers in support of the fact that formal thought was occurring in her "optimally trained" group may be derived from the children already in that age at which Piaget suggest formal thought is possible independent of training. Since no evidence is offered that the levels of thought Taba indicates as "higher" derives from one age group of children in a class rather than another, the evidence that is suggested as indicating that training fostered thinking cannot be properly evaluated. The other point suggested by the age range of Taba's sample is to question the nature of the teaching strategies Taba reports as having been suggested for the young children. It is important to remember that Taba's sample includes three second-grade classes and five third-grade classes. Taba herself writes (a portion of this quotation was cited earlier):

> The early years of school may need to concentrate on providing abundant experiences in manipulation and combining, matching, and grouping objects in order to facilitate the mastery of concrete thinking. Opportunities for the active processing of information may provide the

[32] J. H. Flavell, *The Developmental Psychology of Jean Piaget* (Princeton, N.J.: Van Nostrand Co., 1963), p. 203.
[33] J. H. Flavell, *The Developmental Psychology of Jean Piaget*, p. 204.

necessary conditions for the evolution and organization of abstract conceptual schemes.[34]

Taba speaks in terms of experiences in manipulating and grouping objects, yet she trains her teachers to talk about grouping with children. Thus, it is reported that six- and seven-year-old children are responding to questions about grouping, labeling, and classifying for a period of an hour. It is difficult to conceive of the experience of answering questions as equal to the manipulating, combining, matching, and grouping of objects. Can we consider what Taba describes as her teaching strategies facilitating the mastery of concrete thinking?

Contrast Taba's suggested teaching strategies with that of Peel, a British educator:

> We noted that science, as much as geography and history, could form a rewarding subject for junior school pupils, provided the emphasis was on classifying and finding differences between observable data. Such science should be descriptive. Lastly, problem arithmetic and practical mathematics should make the most of the child's power to classify, serialize and equate.—It follows also from the insistence that thought is internalized action, that experiments, activity, construction, assembly and sorting out of material objects and visible entities are a necessary precursor of thought. This brings us again to the function of primary school education in developing the thinking powers of children. The artificial nature of language and number has been mentioned. It is all the more important therefore that activity and construction form the basis of primary education not only to close the gap between actual thinking levels and the stereotyped use of language and number but also to provide naturally developed surely based foundation for the more abstract formal thinking of adolescence. The primary school child has to reach fully the state of equilibrium of concrete thought before he is ready and equipped to advance to adolescent and adult thought.[35]

At the inception of her study, Taba condemned the current teaching-learning practices for they ". . . tend to cultivate a passive mastery of ideas instead of their active discovery, a tendency to follow the 'recipes' in solving problems instead of analyzing problems and searching for generalizations with which to organize facts and plan an attack on problems.[36] Taba went on to assert:

> Curriculum is seldom organized to focus on active formation and use of abstract ideas. Classroom learning experiences are not usually designed to provide a cumulative sequence of learning cognitive skills which is at once psychologically sound and logically valid.[37]

[34] Hilda Taba and others, "Thinking in Elementary School Children," p. 22.
[35] E. A. Peel, *The Pupil's Thinking* (London: Oldbourne, 1960), p. 10.
[36] Hilda Taba and others, "Thinking in Elementary School Children," p. 2.
[37] *Ibid.*, p. 2.

Having quite clearly expressed her condemnation of passive learning,
Taba, near the conclusion of her study, explains the fact that in the
eighty taped records secured during the course of the study, there
were few children's questions, in the following way:

> The percentage of child seeking is low at all grade levels and for all
> discussions. Since the strategy involved programming the development
> of thought into "digestible steps," fewer questions may have been
> necessary on the part of the children.[38]

[38] *Ibid.*, p. 138.

IX

The Design and Scope of Each Study

Each of the five studies was designed to explore an area of interest to the researcher. The scope of each investigation was determined by many factors—time, place, available resources, and foremost, of course, the needs of the study. Herein are detailed the dimensions and design of each study and the point or points of similarity and difference.

THE LANGUAGE OF THE CLASSROOM

The aim of the initial phase of the Bellack study was to describe the linguistic behavior of teacher and pupils in classroom discussion. Additionally, the questions of the relationship between linguistic behavior and pupil learning and attitude change were to be explored. In order to secure information relevant to these aims, a study was designed that contained the following five procedures:

1. A unit of instruction and analysis was selected. Instruction was to be based upon the first four chapters of Calderwood's pamphlet *International Economic Problems.*

2. Measures of learning and attitude change were developed. These measures consisted of one test of student knowledge and one attitude scale. The test, divided into three sections, asked for definitions, principles of economics, and application of these principles. The test was developed by the research staff on the basis of an analysis of the material in the Calderwood pamphlet. The attitude scale was a seven-point scale that attempted to arrive at the students' attitude toward the study of economics. As initially developed, the attitude scale ran from extremely positive to extremely negative, but, since it was found that the extremely negative statements were not chosen, a revised attitude scale ranging from very positive to relatively neutral attitudes was administered.

The remaining three steps in Bellack's research design will be enumerated here, but discussed in greater detail in those sections dealing with the collection and analysis of information.

3. Data were collected. These data included the pre- and post-tests of knowledge and attitudes. In addition, recordings and transcriptions of classroom verbal behavior were secured.

4. A system of content analysis was developed so that the linguistic behavior of teachers and students could be categorized.

5. The results of the analysis were coded and analyzed statistically.

The aim of the second phase of the Bellack investigation was to analyze further those aspects of classroom verbal behavior that had been designated as "pedagogical moves" during the initial phase of the study. It was Bellack's purpose, in carrying his analysis further, to reveal in a more detailed form the functions these pedagogical moves serve and thus to identify further the rules teachers and pupils follow implicitly. The second phase of the Bellack study was devoted to an expansion of the original system for analysis to include ways of identifying the functions of the four pedagogical moves: soliciting, structuring, responding, and reaction, and the ways in which teachers and pupils discharge these functions in the classroom.

In discussing the design and scope of the Flanders study, recall that the Flanders report deals with two studies: a study designated as a laboratory study and referred to by Flanders as the "first year experiments," and the larger major study referred to by Flanders as the "second year experiments." Flanders' first year laboratory study was designed to study the relationships between controlled teacher influence and the effect of this influence upon dependent behavior among students. It was believed that the laboratory approach would ensure control of students' goal perceptions and the assessment of dependence. It was Flanders' plan to manipulate goal perception because of his belief that the teacher's choice of direct or indirect patterns of influence when goals are ambiguous is crucial to the control of dependent behavior. His theory suggests that, while the natural tendency of teachers is to be direct when goals are unclear, and the natural tendency of students is to be compliant when goals are unclear, these natural tendencies run counter to the conditions necessary for maximum learning.

The first year experiment (see Table II) tested three major hypotheses: (1) Direct teacher influence restricts learning when a student's perception of the goal is confused and ambiguous. (2) Direct teacher influence increases learning when a student's perception of the goal is clear and acceptable. (3) Indirect teacher influence in-

TABLE II
Design of Flanders' First Year Study

Goal Manipulation \ Teachers' Behavior	Direct Influence by the Teacher	Indirect Influence by the Teacher
The learning task is initially ambiguous	Treatment I Each group size 20 balanced for I. Q. and sex	Treatment II Each group size 20 balanced for I. Q. and sex
The learning task is initially clear	Treatment III Each group size 20 balanced for I. Q. and sex	Each group size 20 balanced for I. Q. and sex

From Ned A. Flanders, "Teacher Influence, Pupil Attitudes, and Achievement," p. 23.

creases learning when a student's perception of the goal is confused and ambiguous:

> It was proposed that the analysis of any data relevant to the support or rejection of these hypotheses be analyzed separately for gifted, average, and below average students.[1]
>
> Four experimental treatments comprised the first year design. In one-half of the groups a direct pattern of teacher influence was created. In the other one-half an indirect pattern of teacher influence was used. The variable of teacher influence was manipulated by having a member of the research staff, who was an experienced teacher, practice controlling his behavior until he could present a consistent pattern of influence in spontaneous interaction.
>
> The second independent variable was the student's perception of the learning goal. In one-half of the groups a condition of goal ambiguity was induced, and in the other half, a condition of goal clarity was induced.[2]

This same design was used for 560 students who worked on a geometry learning task and 480 students who worked on a social studies task. In the geometry experiments, seven groups of twenty students were exposed to each treatment. In the social studies experiment, six groups of twenty students were exposed to each treatment.

The length of the experiment for both groups was two hours and ten minutes and the sequence was the same. An outline of the experimental session is shown in Table III.

[1] Ned A. Flanders, "Teacher Influence, Pupil Attitudes, and Achievement: Studies in Interaction Analysis," U.S. Office of Education Cooperative Research Project No. 397 (Minneapolis: University of Minnesota, 1960), p. 19.
[2] *Ibid.*, p. 22.

TABLE III
Outline of Flanders' Experimental Session

Period	Length	Test or Questionnaire	Other Activities
I	50 min.	Booklet I—Achievement pre-test of content Booklet II—Dependence proneness personality test	Orientation of students to experiment
II	15 min.		Teacher explanation establishing goal perception as clear or ambiguous. Tape-recorded lecture introducing content in clear or ambiguous style.
III	15 min.	Booklet III—first test of tendency to dependent behavior. First goal perception measure.	
IV	15 min.		Teacher-pupil discussion of the content, teacher influence either direct or indirect.
V	10 min.	Booklet IV—second test of tendency to dependent behavior. Second goal perception measure. Measure of student's perception of teacher influence.	
VI	10 min.		Work period for seat work with individual worksheet.
VII	15 min.	Booklet V—Second test of student's perception of teacher influence. Third test of dependent tendencies. Booklet VI—Achievement post-test of content.	

From Ned. A. Flanders, "Teacher Influence, Pupil Attitudes, and Achievement," p. 24.

In the second year study, two-week units of work in mathematics and social studies were prepared and taught by thirty-two teachers. The teacher influence was measured through interaction patterns. Student achievement was measured by pre- and post-tests and the materials of instruction were kept constant, since they were supplied by the staff.

A six-step procedure characterized the second year's study:

1. Curriculum units that could be adapted to use for all children in both mathematics and social studies had to be selected.
2. Selection of teachers had to be decided so that the natural style of some would be direct while the natural style of others would be indirect.
3. Units of study had to be built. Enough material for thirty-five to forty students that could be used by teachers of different styles was prepared. Material was prepared that would be appropriate for fast and slow readers.
4. Observers were trained in the technique of interaction analysis.
5. Thirty-two units of study were scheduled so that the three observers could be assigned to the first two days of every unit, the last few days, and have additional visits in between.
6. All data were punched on to I.B.M. cards and analyzed.

ASSESSMENT OF THE QUALITY OF TEACHING

Hughes, at the beginning of her study, states that her interest was centered in *good teaching*. Her study was focused on classroom life, the interaction of the teacher with one child, with a group of children, and with the total class. Believing that the center of classroom influence is the teacher, Hughes suggests that the teachers' attitudes, processes, and functions affect not only the activities of the class, the degree of children's participation, the mental processes they utilize in their work, but even their attitudes toward one another. Thus, in analyzing the classroom records of teacher-pupil interaction in terms of the functions performed by the teacher, Hughes sought to picture classroom life.

Hughes designed her study by posing six questions, which were to be explored and answered through the course of the research project:

1. What differences in pattern of teacher acts (functions) may be found among elementary teachers *judged* as good teachers?
2. What teaching acts are dominant or statistically more frequent among good teachers than among those less adequate?
3. What differences in teaching behavior exist among selected teaching situations, i.e., reading, activity or work period, or a developmental lesson in social studies or arithmetic?
4. What teaching acts or combination of teaching acts appear to stimulate use of highest mental processes, personal involvement, and creativity on the part of the children?
5. How do children view the teacher-learner situation?

6. What is good teaching? What is the rationale that supports the model of good teaching?[3]

A STUDY OF THE LOGIC OF TEACHING

The focus of the first phase of the Smith study was the nature of "logical operations." As defined by Smith, "logical operations" are the forms verbal behavior takes as the teacher shapes the subject matter for instruction.

The design of the first phase consisted of three parts:

1. The collection of tape recordings of the high school classes in the conventional content fields—science, English, social studies, and mathematics.
2. The designation of a unit of analysis. This unit, as developed, was the episode. The episode begins with an expression that initiates a verbal exchange and ends when the discussion of the topic has been completed. Also identified was a unit of discourse called the monologue. A monologue consists of a unit of verbal behavior of one individual.
3. The final step was the development of categories by which to sort episodes. Episodes were classified by their opening remarks or entries. Their logical character could most satisfactorily be determined by reference to the response it demanded.

The focus of the second phase of the Smith study was on teaching strategies. Strategies, as defined by Smith, are concerned with attaining content objectives. In the course of the second study, different units of analysis were identified and criteria were developed for their analysis, then:

1. Ventures were identified. Ventures are described as units of discourse having a central point, a theme that pervades the exchange.
2. Nine types of ventures were identified: causal, conceptual, evaluative, informatory, interpretive, procedural, reason, rule, and system.
3. Two dimensions of strategy were identified: treatment and control. In analyzing the treatment factor of strategy, the concept of "move" as a kind of verbal manipulation in identifying and describing the treatment dimension was defined.
4. Conceptual ventures were then further analyzed into eighteen moves.

[3] Marie M. Hughes and Associates, "The Assessment of the Quality of Teaching: A Research Report," U.S. Office of Education Cooperative Research Project No. 353 (Salt Lake City: University of Utah, 1959), p. 10.

5. Finally, an analysis of four kinds of strategies, based on the compositions of moves they involve, was developed.

THINKING IN ELEMENTARY SCHOOL CHILDREN

The central focus of the Taba study was the examination of the development of thought under optimum training conditions. Working in the area of the social studies, Taba developed her study in the following sequence:

1. A curriculum was designed around basic ideas as targets for learning.
2. Specially selected teachers were given special instructions to ensure that proper teaching strategies were used and that they understood the objectives of the study.
3. A test of the children's ability to draw inferences, called the *Social Studies Inference Test*, was developed.
4. A category system for coding classroom discourse was developed, as well as a method of representing verbal discourse graphically.

   A secondary objective of the Taba study was to examine the effect on the development of cognitive processes of such factors as ability, age, and cultural background.

SUMMARY

In analyzing the design and scope of these five studies and the ways in which they are similar and the ways in which they differ, it is obvious that all five researchers have worked to develop a category system that would accurately and objectively portray classroom life. While the development of such a system was the central task of Bellack, Hughes and Smith's project, Flanders' and Hughes' work has a different and perhaps further emphasis. For Flanders and Hughes the category system is a tool of investigation. Thus Flanders uses his system in the only hypothesis testing study among the five studies. Although Taba indicates at the inception of her study that its purpose is to view the effects of specialized training on the growth of student thinking, suggesting that she, like Flanders, is engaged in a hypothesis testing study, the absence of both a control group and standardized norms for measuring this growth makes it clear that no hypothesis testing is involved. Thus while the Taba study moves toward the use of the category system as a tool in a manner similar to Flanders', it is not the clear hypothesis testing investigation that the Flanders study is.

X

Styles and Systems of Observation Used in Each Study

Direct observation is the oldest, and remains the commonest, instrument of scientific research.[1]

The major assumption in research work that employs observers or technical observational equipment, or both, is that the effect of observation upon those observed will not significantly affect the results of the observation:

> The presence of an observer might be expected to produce self-consciousness or other reactions that would distort the behavior which is being studied but this factor has usually been found to be less serious than might be anticipated. Observers repeatedly report that much-observed children, as well as adults, seem quite readily to become habituated to the presence of an outsider. The observer normally is careful not to participate in the activities he is observing unless in so doing he deliberately is introducing a factor pertinent to his study. Instances have, however, been reported in which the children's behavior seems to have been influenced, at least for a time, by the observer's presence, and a teacher or parent whose practices are being observed would be less than human if he were not somewhat affected although the passage of time here also has a tranquilizing effect. Whatever the observer's effect may be, it is not likely to be so pronounced that the records fail to show individual differences.[2]

Researchers who are concerned about this possible effect of observers on those being observed seek to mitigate the observer effect through appropriate measures. Thus Bellack writes:

> It was realized that the presence of a tape recorder and the teachers' and students' knowledge that they were participating in a research study would probably influence their behavior. Instructions were therefore designed to minimize this interference. The instructions to the teacher, for example, reassured them that the reserach did not involve

[1] Arthur T. Jersild and Margaret F. Meigs, "Direct Observation as a Research Method," *Review of Educational Research*, 9:472, December, 1939.
[2] *Ibid.*, p. 481.

an evaluation of their performance and that complete anonymity would be maintained.[3]

Hughes also discussed this problem in her report:

> It is impossible to assess the effects of the presence of observers. All teachers had the schedule of observations several days in advance. In most cases, they had designated the time they wished and the principal had incorporated their preference in the schedule.[4]

In Smith's study he reports that, at the inception of his study, he wrote to the school superintendent of the participating schools to outline the purposes of his project. In this letter Smith discussed the possible effect of observation upon the teachers involved in his study and discussed the steps that would be taken to lessen this effect:

> 3. Teachers whose classes are to be taped will be given the following facts about the recordings:
>   a. The researcher's work is merely to observe and describe. No evaluation whatsoever is to be made of any teacher's teaching or of the conduct of his or her classroom activities. This is a fact to be stressed, since some of the teachers might work under taping conditions with self-consciousness and tensions which knowledge of this fact would dispel.
>   b. Teachers, classes, and schools will remain anonymous on the tapes and on the verbatim transcriptions of these tapes, being identified thereon only by code letters and numbers. Only project staff members may listen to these tapes.
>   c. Individual teachers, schools, and cooperating officials will be officially and gratefully credited for their part in this research on the final report of this project when it is published.[5]

In his study Flanders writes:

> We have studiously avoided any reference to teacher evaluation in soliciting the cooperation of teachers in our research. We have achieved teacher cooperation by emphasizing that our major concern is the analysis of teacher-pupil contacts and that there are so many different kinds of learning activities, so many styles of teaching and so many types of pupils, that a great deal of research will be necessary before teaching effectiveness can be evaluated.[6]

---

[3] Arno A. Bellack et al., *The Language of the Classroom*, p. 11.

[4] Marie M. Hughes and Associates, "The Assessment of the Quality of Teaching: A Research Report," U.S. Office of Education Cooperative Research Project No. 353 (Salt Lake City: University of Utah, 1959), p. 38.

[5] B. Othanel Smith and Milton O. Meux, "A Study of the Logic of Teaching" (Urbana: Bureau of Educational Research, College of Education, University of Illinois, 1963), p. 201.

[6] Ned A. Flanders, "Teacher Influence, Pupil Attitudes, and Achievement: Studies in Interaction Analysis," U.S. Office of Education Cooperative Research Project No. 397 (Minneapolis: University of Minnesota, 1960), Appendix F, p. 30.

In addition to indicating the measures taken to mitigate observer effect on those observed, the quotations of Bellack, Flanders, and Smith state their belief that teachers' cooperation with researchers will be more easily secured if evaluation is not the intent of the researcher.

Hughes is the only researcher who attempted to gain some empirical evidence on the effect of observation upon the teachers:

> We held the hypothesis that teachers who felt nervous might be more active during the initial visits; therefore, the records were examined to determine whether or not a teacher performed more functions (acts) during the first thirty-minute observation. No relationship to order of observation was found.[7]

The subjective opinions of the researchers seem to support the assumption that observer effect is minimal. Thus Bellack states:

> Observations during the data collection and subsequent analyses of the data indicated a remarkably high degree of cooperation both from teacher and from students. Although it cannot be assumed that the research procedures had no effect on the classroom behavior, it seems reasonable to conclude that this effect was minimal.[8]

Hughes, too, reports upon the good rapport between researcher and teacher:

> The observers were trained school people who had learned to be unobtrusive in their record taking. Many teachers commented about their pleasantness, skill, and business-like manner as they went about their work.[9]

Smith, in his letter to the participating school superintendents, wrote the following, obviously based on his previous experience with classroom observation:

> d. To record a class session requires two individuals to handle equipment and to record the non-verbal context of the proceedings. The project staff had found that the presence of these individuals (graduate students on the project staff) has created no discernible distrubance or disruption of classroom activity. After the first day, their presence was generally taken for granted and the normal atmosphere of the class reasserted itself.[10]

The problem of observer effect is a nagging one and cannot be dismissed too lightly. However, as Medley and Mitzel indicate, there

---

[7] Marie M. Hughes and Associates, "The Assessment of the Quality of Teaching," p. 38.

[8] Arno A. Bellack et al., *The Language of the Classroom*, p. 11.

[9] Marie M. Hughes and Associates, "The Assessment of the Quality of Teaching," p. 38.

[10] B. Othanel Smith and Milton O. Meux, "A Study of the Logic of Teaching," p. 202, Appendix 1.

is either information derived from observation with the risk of bias or no information at all:

> The objection that teachers and pupils may not behave in exactly the same way when observers are present as they behave when no observer is present has no completely satisfactory answer. The problem of comparing observed and unobserved behavior is akin to that of a small boy who turned out the bedroom light but could never quite make it to his bed before the room got dark. To know how teachers and pupils behave while they are under observation seems better than to know nothing at all about how teachers and pupils behave.[11]

None of these studies attempted a random sample of observations, that is, sampling either teacher or class at random times throughout the day, month, or year. The nonrandomness of the sample simplified the research design and doubtlessly lessened teacher observational anxiety, but also limits the use that can be made of the observational data.

Dewey wrote in 1933:

> All the instrumentalities of observation—the various meters and graphs and scopes—fulfill a part of their scientific role in helping to eliminate meanings supplied because of habit, prejudice, the strong momentary preoccupation of excitement and anticipation and by the vogue of existing theories. Photographs, phonographs, kymographs, actinographs, seismographs, plethysographs and the like, moreover, give records that are permanent, so that they can be employed by different persons and by the same person in different states of mind: i.e., under the influence of varying expectations and dominant beliefs. Thus purely personal presuppositions (due to habit, to desire, to after-effects of recent experience) may be largely eliminated. In ordinary language the facts are *objective* rather than *subjectively* determined. In this way tendencies to premature interpretation are held in check.[12]

Bellack, Smith, and Taba all collected their material by tape recording classes. The position supported here is that much of the content of the speech act is lost when verbal behavior is categorized from a tape recorder. However, as indicated in the quotation from Dewey, tape recordings, like other permanent records, have very great advantages. Just as theoretically unencumbered category systems lend themselves to manipulation from many different points of view, so also does the taped class record. The taped class record makes possible the coding and repeated recodings of classroom behavior from as many different perspectives as would be necessary in order to gain insight into the *whys* of classroom behavior.

[11] Donald Medley and Harold E. Mitzel, "Measuring Classroom Behavior by Systematic Observation," in N. L. Gage, ed., American Educational Research Association *Handbook of Research on Teaching* (Chicago: Rand McNally, 1963), p. 248.

[12] John Dewey, *How We Think*, rev. ed. (Boston: D. C. Heath and Co., 1933), p. 172.

Hughes' method of observation, stenographic records of class-room behavior, is quite similar to tape recordings in that no attempt is made to categorize information, but simply to get a record of what transpires in the classroom. Hughes enumerates the advantages of the specimen stenographic recording; these advantages may be said to hold equally well for the taped recordings:

> First, such records enable us to "hold teaching still" in a perma-nent form so that it may be studied and its distinctive quality and characteristics identified. One can read and reread a specimen record of teacher-behavior until the children and teacher who are interacting within the situation come alive.
>
> Second, the behavior phenomena and situation are secured at the time of occurrence.
>
> Third, the interdependence and the complexities of behavior and situation are more often than not preserved. It is possible to trace through an interaction with a given child from the first minute of the record to the last minute although dozens of interactions with other children intervene.
>
> Fourth, the continuity of the teacher's behavior is retained.
>
> Fifth, the specimen record of teacher-behavior is theoretically neutral. No judgment is made in regard to what is taking place. The record itself mirrors exactly what happens, rather than what anyone thought about the episodes.
>
> Sixth, the permanency of the record makes it possible to examine it through the use of any number of conceptual formulations. It may be examined for different purposes by those with differing interests. It may be looked at in its entirety or examined interaction by interaction. More than anything else, the specimen record of teacher-behavior pro-vides an intimate picture of the classroom in its day-by-day reality.[13]

In the Hughes study the directions to the classroom observers are reported. A small portion of this material that deals with nonverbal behavior has already been quoted here:

> You are to focus your attention upon the teacher and what he says and does. To the extent possible, record his non-verbal behavior. Make sure that you secure as much as possible of what the children say to one another when in interaction with the teacher. It is of crucial importance to get the child's statement or action that prompts the response of the teacher and, in turn, to secure the child's response to the teacher. The *to whom* the teacher is speaking should be made explicit. When chil-dren's names are not heard, child 1, child 2, etc. may be used.
>
> You will find it necessary to follow the teacher about the room in order to hear what he says. Immediately after taking the record, fill in your shorthand and abbreviations so that you can read the record, then collate your record with your partner in observation. *Retain in the final record only that upon which you both agree.*[14]

---

[13] Marie M. Hughes and Associates, "The Assessment of the Quality of Teaching," p. 36.

[14] *Ibid.*, p. 39.

Hughes concludes her discussion of the observational procedure with a discussion of reliability, observer bias, and other observational problems:

> Two and one-half years of previous experience with record-taking had demonstrated to us the rapidity and the variety of action in the classroom. We found the record-taking method as described to be adequate. In our earlier efforts to determine reliability of two observers, we found that it stabilized between 65 and 75 per cent of agreement. Examination of the data demonstrated that the differences could be located in episodes where one observer recorded the first part of the action and the other observer the latter part. Therefore, collation of records resulted in a more adequate record.
>
> The field staff could take only one record each half-day. Even that was too strenuous day after day so that one record a day for a pair had to be scheduled once or twice a week.
>
> To control bias, no pair took a second record until they had gone through a cycle of pairing and no pair took a second record on a teacher. The large number of records were taken by the four regular staff members, thus forming six pairings. One week, a Provo staff member of equal experience substituted for one of the regular staff members. This formed six new pairings. For one record, the chief investigator substituted; therefore, eleven pairings are represented in the one hundred and five records.[15]

The procedure for gathering the taped recordings in the Smith study is described as follows:

> The recording equipment consisted of a tape recorder running at 3-3/4 feet per second with a seven-inch reel of tape. We had a volume unit (VU″) meter installed in place of the recording level eye in order to better control the lower volumes. A pair of headphones was also used for a direct aural check of the recording while it was being made. Three semi-directional microphones were used, each with its own adjustable stand. A felt pad to lessen the pickup of jarring noises was placed under each microphone stand. The three microphones fed into a microphone mixer which had individual volume controls and two amplification stages. This device enabled the person recording to turn on only the microphone closest to the person speaking. This did much to increase the intelligibility of the voice by decreasing background noise.[16]

Smith reports that five consecutive class periods for seventeen teachers were taped. Of these, two sets of observations or ten individual class sessions in ninth grade mathematics were useless for purposes of analysis because the amount of classroom seat work rendered them unintelligible. In addition, one set of five individual observations for a ninth grade science class was useless because the

[15] *Ibid.*, p. 39

[16] B. Othanel Smith and Milton O. Meux, "A Study of the Logic of Teaching," p. 209.

tapes were reported as inaudible. Thus, fifteen of the eighty-five tapes, or 17.6 per cent of the attempted observations, were totally useless. Smith does not indicate what percentage of the remaining 82.4 per cent of the tapes were successfully used in analysis. Smith attempts no explanation for the fact that all recording difficulties are concentrated at the same grade level. There is also little to account for the fact that five consecutive recordings in ninth grade science were all inaudible. Whatever the cause, the effect was to change the sampling of ninth grade classes from five sets of observations of twenty-five individual classes to two sets of observations of ten individual classes, thus reducing the proportion of ninth grade observations from 29.4 per cent of the total to 11.7 per cent of the total.

Bellack and Taba reported no such difficulty with their taped observations. Indeed, Taba reports no information at all about her tape recordings. Except for the need to switch from a nondirectional microphone placed on the teacher's desk to a microphone worn by the teacher to promote greater fidelity of recording, no difficulties were reported by Bellack in securing his tapes. The tapes were gathered in the following manner, after the microphone switch:

> Subsequent classes, therefore, were recorded by means of a microphone worn by the teacher and a microphone placed among the students, both of which were fed into a Switchcraft 301 TR mixer which was, in turn, connected to a T-1500 Wollensak tape recorder. The tape recorder, placed at the side of the classroom, was operated by a technician attached to the project staff.[17]

Bellack reports on the percentage of the classroom observation transcribed:

> Typescript protocols of the tape recordings were prepared. These typescripts were then revised by a second person who audited the tape recording and made whatever corrections and additions were necessary. At this point, over 95 per cent of the classroom discourse was transcribed, but as a further check on accuracy of the transcriptions, the recordings were audited once again when the protocols were analyzed. In the final analysis, probably no more than three or four per cent of the classroom discussion was missed, and this material primarily involved instances in which several students spoke simultaneously for very brief periods of time.[18]

Bellack's report of missing only 3 to 4 per cent of the discourse, as compared to Hughes' 65 to 75 per cent agreement on stenographic records, indicates the greater fidelity possible when tape recordings of classroom behavior are used. However, Smith's total loss of plus 17 per cent of his recordings indicates that tape recordings too can be a great deal less than perfect as recording instruments. Since

[17] Arno A. Bellack et al., *The Language of the Classroom*, p. 11.
[18] *Ibid.*, p. 12.

Smith does not report how much of the remaining plus 82 per cent of his recordings were lost, we cannot compare the fidelity of the Smith recordings with the Hughes stenographic records. However, if Smith's fidelity on the remaining plus 82 per cent was as good as Bellack's, even the loss of fifteen complete observational records would give Smith greater overall recording fidelity than those attained by Hughes' stenographic records.

Of all the studies the only one that can be said to have a system for observation is Flanders'. The other studies might more properly be spoken of as having a method of observation. The observers who use Flanders' category system categorize verbal statements at three-second intervals into one of ten categories (Table IV). They record the number that best represents what they have observed in sequence

TABLE IV

Flanders' Categories for Interaction Analysis

TEACHER TALK	Indirect Influence	1. ACCEPTS FEELING: accepts and clarifies the feeling tone of the students in a nonthreatening manner. Feelings may be positive or negative. Predicting or recalling feelings are included. 2. PRAISES OR ENCOURAGES: praises or encourages student action or behavior. Jokes that release tension, not at the expense of another individual, nodding head or saying "um hm?" or "go on" are included. 3. ACCEPTS OR USES IDEAS OF STUDENT: clarifying, building, or developing ideas suggested by a student. As teacher brings more of his own ideas into play, shift to category five. 4. ASKS QUESTIONS: asking a question about content or procedure with the intent that a student answer.
	Direct Influence	5. LECTURING: giving facts or opinions about content or procedure; expressing his own ideas, asking rhetorical questions. 6. GIVING DIRECTIONS: directions, commands, or orders to which a student is expected to comply. 7. CRITICIZING OR JUSTIFYING AUTHORITY: statements intended to change student behavior from nonacceptable to acceptable pattern; bawling someone out; stating why the teacher is doing what he is doing; extreme self-reference.
STUDENT TALK		8. STUDENT TALK—RESPONSE: talk by students in response to teacher. Teacher initiates the contact or solicits student statement. 9. STUDENT TALK—INITIATION: talk by students which they initiate. If "calling on" student is only to indicate who may talk next, observer must decide whether student wanted to talk. If he did, use this category.
		10. SILENCE OR CONFUSION: pauses, short periods of silence and periods of confusion in which communication cannot be understood by the observer.

From Ned A. Flanders, "Teacher Influence, Pupil Attitudes, and Achievement," Appendix F. p. 5.

in a column. Flanders instructs his observers to draw a double line in this column of numbers when there is a major shift in class formation, communication patterns, or subject matter. The numbers recorded between double lines are called episodes. After observations are made, episodes, or series of episodes, can be tabulated onto a 10 × 10 matrix. The tabulation and recording of Flanders' material will be treated in the section on categories of analysis.

Whether immediate coding on the basis of observation is preferable to coding after an observation record has been made can be debated. However, for reasons similar to those already quoted from Dewey's *How We Think* and from Hughes' rationale for the use of specimen records, the coding of behavior after recording seems to be the more generally accepted position although suitable acknowledgment is made of the difficulties inherent in either approach:

> The choice between predetermined categories and the "running account" type of record has been made, in part at least, on the basis of the investigator's purpose. The former procedure has been found expedient when the intention is to obtain a quantitative survey of the frequencies of certain clearly definable and psychologically distinguishable forms of behavior. The disadvantages, of course, are that once units have been decided upon, the observer is not free to adapt his account to what he observes; rather he must fit what he observes to his categories and this sometimes may mean that he is compelled to project his own definitions on the behavior that he sees. In the running account, the worker, in devising his final scheme for treating the data, can capitalize on the contents of his records as well as upon incidental learnings during the course of his observations. Both procedures involve the danger of shifts of emphasis during the course of the study, and neither is proof against the development of bias on the observer's part during the study. [19]
>
> There are a number of advantages to having the interviewer or the observer code the data. For one thing, he is in a position to notice the situation as well as the individual's behavior. Thus, he has more information upon which to base a judgment than the coder working from the written record. Another advantage is that categorization by the data collector saves both time and labor.
>
> Notwithstanding these advantages, categorization of complex data is usually done by coders after the data have been collected. This procedure allows time for reflection; on-the-spot judgments of an interviewer or observer may not be as discerning as judgments made with more time for deliberation. The judgments of data collectors may be colored by irrelevancies such as the appearance and mannerisms of the respondent, his accent, responses to previous questions, etc. Moreover, if each interviewer or observer categorizes only the data he collects, unreliability is likely to be increased. There is a tendency to develop a frame of reference with respect to the material that one is coding. Even

[19] Arthur T. Jersild and Margaret F. Meigs, "Direct Observation as a Research Method," p. 477.

if the data collectors were all perfectly consistent with one another in their use of categories initially—an unlikely assumption—they would tend to develop varying frames of reference appropriate to their limited materials, which would make their categorizations unreliable after a time. A common frame of reference is easier to obtain and check in an office coding operation than in the field.[20]

It is, of course, important to note that there is no particular reason why Flanders' system could not be used in categorizing material that had been tape recorded. Flanders reports on the reliability of his coding system:

> Training of both old and new observers took place prior to the teaching of the first unit of study. During the first part of this training the new members of the team achieved Scott reliability ratings which ranged from 0.64 to 0.76. With additional training these ratings improved until the between-observer Scott reliabilities were consistently above 0.85.
>
> Throughout the data-collecting period the observers met together about once a week. At these meetings any unusual classification problems were discussed and a policy established so that if other observers faced the same problems later on they could react consistently.
>
> In May of the second year, the two substitute observers and one of the regular observers had the opportunity to check their reliability approximately two months after the last regularly scheduled observation. Although this was in connection with another study, it presented the opportunity of checking on reliability after a period of inactivity. The three Scott indexes were 0.87, 0.90, and 0.94.[21]
>
> The case for adequate observer reliability rests on measures of reliability and the possible bias that could have occurred through assignment. Reliability checks after training indicated Scott indexes above 0.85 and group discussions were held regularly to discuss unusual problems of classification. The evidence indicates that the observers could make distinctions necessary to differentiate between patterns of teacher influence.[22]

Herbert and Swayze report on an interesting extension of tape recorded classroom observations through use of dual track recording: one track picks up the classroom interaction in a manner similar to that used by Bellack, Smith, and Taba while the other track can be used for either an observer's running commentary or children's conversations.

> With a wireless microphone an FM receiver and a stereophonic tape recorder, we found, an observer can obtain a full clear and permanent

[20] Claire Selltiz, Marie Jahoda, Morton Deutsch, and Stuart W. Cook, *Research Methods in Social Relations* (New York: Holt, Rinehart, and Winston, 1963), p. 402.
[21] Ned A. Flanders, "Teacher Influence, Pupil Attitudes, and Achievement," p. 48.
[22] *Ibid.*, p. 49.

record of almost any activity in almost any setting. During classroom observations we were able to record every word teachers spoke, every sound they made and almost every sound within their hearing even when the teacher spoke too softly or the children moved about too noisily to permit an observer in the room to make out what was being said. To fill out and help interpret the information obtained in this way, we were able to synchronize with the recording of classroom sounds a spoken description by an observer of non-audible events—movements and gestures of teachers and pupils, seating arrangements, writing on blackboards, the showing of pictures, maps and slides. These matched recordings, made on two channels of a two track tape, could be played back separately or together, at any time, and as often as needed for purposes of analysis and interpretation.[23]

Recently Simon and Boyer published a compilation of recently developed systems of observation. Though they detail twenty-five such systems they report that over fifty such systems exist.[24]

[23] John Herbert and John Swayze, "Wireless Observation," Horace Mann-Lincoln Institute of School Experimentation (New York: Bureau of Publication, Teachers College, Columbia University, 1964), p. 1.

[24] Anita Simon and E. Gill Boyer, "Mirrors for Behavior" (Philadelphia: Temple University, 1968).

XI

Categories of Analysis and Statistical Systems Used in Each Study

The category systems used in the five studies will be compared and the similarities and differences between and among them will be pursued. At this juncture the analysis of the five category systems will be presented along with their reliability estimates, as well as the patterns of analysis used in each study. A discussion of the results of these analyses will be presented when question seven is discussed. In some instances, a discussion of the analysis system cannot be easily pursued without reference to the results. In those cases, the results will be presented within this chapter.

THE LANGUAGE OF THE CLASSROOM

The central concept in the development of the category system in the first part of the Bellack study is the pedagogical move. As discussed earlier, Bellack suggests that classroom discourse can be helpfully analyzed into two groups of pedagogical moves: the initiatory and the reflexive. Each group contains two different kinds of moves. The structuring and the soliciting moves are the initiatory moves and the reacting and responding are the reflexive moves.

Bellack reports his reliability for identification of these four pedagogical moves and indicates how this reliability was derived:

> Four members of the research staff participated in the reliability test. Twelve five-page samples were selected at random from protocols of six different teachers . . . . The four coders were divided into two teams. Assignment of coders to the two coding teams was rotated so that all possible permutations of team membership were compared. Following our general procedures for analysis, one member of each team coded a given sample, the other member reviewed the coding, both members of each team then arbitrated any disagreements between the initial coder and the reviewer.
>
> After each of the 12 samples has been coded independently by the

two teams, the codings of the teams were compared, and the percentage of agreement was computed in terms of both number of lines and number of moves.[1]

The results of the reliability estimates are presented in Table V.

TABLE V
Bellack's Reliability Pedagogical Moves

Major Categories	Per Cent Agreement Moves	Per Cent Agreement Lines
Pedagogical moves	94	93
Substantive meanings	95	96
Substantive-logical meanings	88	91
Instructional meanings	88	91
Instructional-logical meanings	87	84

From Arno A. Bellack et al., *The Language of the Classroom*, p. 35.

Bellack's pedagogical move is analyzed in terms of eight dimensions as shown below.

Each pedagogical move is coded as follows:[2]

(1) / (2) / (3) / (4) / (5) / (6) / (7) / (8)

(1) Speaker
(2) Type of Pedagogical Move
(3) Substantive Meaning
(4) Substantive-Logical Meaning
(5) Number of Typescript Lines in (3) and (4)
(6) Instructional Meaning
(7) Instructional-Logical Meaning
(8) Number of Typescript Lines in (6) and (7)

Bellack's system for analysis is summarized below:

(1) Speaker: indicates source of utterance
   Teacher (T); *Pupil* (P); *Audio-Visual Device* (A)
(2) Type of Pedagogical Move: reference to function of move
   Initiatory Moves:
      Structuring (STR): sets context for subsequent behavior, launches, halts/excludes
      Soliciting (SOL): directly elicits verbal, physical or mental response
   Reflexive Moves:
      Responding (RES) fulfils expectation of solicitation
      Reacting (REA) modifies and/or rates
      Not Codable (NOC): function uncertain because tape inaudible

[1] Arno A. Bellack et al., *The Language of the Classroom*, p. 35.
[2] *Ibid.*, p. 16.

(3) Substantive Meaning: reference to subject matter topic (based on a content analysis of the pamphlet by Calderwood)

   Trade (TRA)
   Factors of Production and/or Specialization (FSP)
   Import and/or Exports (IMX)

(4) Substantive-Logical Meaning: reference to cognitive process involved in dealing with the subject matter under study

   Analytic Process: use of language or established rules of logic
   Empirical Process: sense experience as criterion of truth
   Evaluative Process: set of criteria or value system as basis for verification

(5) Number of Typescript Lines in (3) and (4) Above

(6) Instructional Meanings: reference to factors related to classroom management

   Assignment (ASG):
   Material (MAT):
   Person (PER):
   Statement (STA)
   Logical Process (LOG):
   Action-General (ACT):
   Action-Vocal (ACV):
   Action-Physical (ACP):
   Action-Cognitive (ACC):
   Action-Emotional (ACE):
   Language Mechanics (LAM)

(7) Instructional-Logical Meaning: reference to cognitive processes related to the distinctly didactic verbal moves in the instructional situation

   Analytic Process:
      Defining-General (DEF)
      Interpreting (INT)
   Empirical Process:
      Fact-Stating (FAC)
      Explaining (XPL)
   Evaluative Process
      Opining (OPN)
      Justifying (JUS)
   Rating: reference to metacommunication; usually an evaluative reaction (REA)
      Positive (POS):
      Admitting (ADM):
      Repeating (RPT):

  Qualifying (QAL):
  Not Admitting (NAD):
  Negative (NEG):
  Extralogical Process
  Performing (PRF)
  Directing (DIR)
  Extralogical Process Not Clear (NCL)
(8) Number of Typescript Lines in (6) and (7) above[3]

Bellack calculated the percentage of lines and moves to reveal such relationships as the kinds and types of teacher pedagogical moves and pupil pedagogical moves, as well as the total number of such moves. The observed regularities of pedagogical moves led Bellack to combine these moves into patterns called teaching cycles. Twenty-one teaching cycles were identified as follows:

1. STR					
2. STR	SOL				
3. STR	REA				
4. STR	REA	REA			
5. STR	SOL	RES			
6. STR	SOL	RES	RES		
7. STR	SOL	REA			
8. STR	SOL	REA	REA ...		
9. STR	SOL	RES	REA ...		
10. STR	SOL	RES	REA	REA ...	
11. STR	SOL	RES	REA	RES ...	
12. STR	SOL	RES	REA	RES ...	REA ...
13. SOL					
14. SOL	RES				
15. SOL	RES	RES ...			
16. SOL	REA				
17. SOL	REA	REA ...			
18. SOL	RES	REA			
19. SOL	RES	REA	REA ...		
20. SOL	RES	REA	RES ...		
21. SOL	RES	REA	RES ...	REA ...	

LEGEND: STR Structuring   RES Responding
      SOL Soliciting   REA Reacting
      ... one or more additional moves of the kind designated[4]

This larger unit of analysis was, in turn, analyzed to ascertain the rate, source, and pattern of classroom discourse.

  The first study also presented comparisons on pre- and post-tests of knowledge and attitude. The average ratings on the valence, activity, and strength dimension of emotional meaning for each class and for each session were prepared.

[3] *Ibid.*, p. 38.
[4] *Ibid.*, p. 195.

The second half of the Bellack study included both the development of a more detailed analysis of the pedagogical move and the combining of teaching cycles by the statistical device of Markov chains for further analysis. Thus, the soliciting move, which had been identified in the first study as accounting for 33.2 per cent of the moves and 22.6 per cent of the lines, was the first of the four pedagogical moves to be analyzed in detail in the second study. A summary of the soliciting act's coding is shown below.

THE PERSONS INVOLVED IN THE SOLICITING-RESPONDING ACT

1. The solicitor
   1.1. The teacher
   1.2. The pupil
   1.3. Any other speaker
2. The agent solicited
   2.1. The teacher
   2.2. All pupils
   2.3. Any one pupil
   2.4. One specified pupil
   2.5. One selected pupil

THE INDICATIVE MEANING OF THE SOLICITING MOVE

1. Pedagogical task
   1.1. Substantive
   1.2. Instructional
2. Type of behavior expected
3. The primary activities
   3.1 Logical process activity
      3.11 The analytic mode
      3.12 The empirical mode
      3.13 The evaluative mode
      3.14 The extra-logical mode
   3.2 The information process activity
      3.21 Assigning a truth function
      3.22 Selecting from stated alternatives
      3.23 Constructing
      3.24 Constructing/assigning
      3.25 Selecting/assigning
4. Clues regarding appropriate terms
   4.1 Terms
   4.2 Terms excluded

4.3 Terms of parallel nature
4.4 Leading
4.5 Propositional functions
5. Occasion for the solicited performance
    5.1 Immediate and within the classroom
    5.2 Immediate and outside the classroom
    5.3 Future of the class session and within classroom
    5.4 Future class session and within classroom
    5.5 Future after class and outside classroom
    5.6 Future unspecified and within classroom
    5.7 Future unspecified and outside classroom

THE STYLISTIC MEANING OF THE SOLICITING MOVE

1. The length of the presentation
2. Mode of presentation
    2.1 The imperative mode
    2.2 The interrogative mode
    2.3 The declarative mode
3. The construction of the move
    3.1 Elliptical
    3.2 Conditional
    3.3 Completion
    3.4 Interlarded information
4. The composition of the move

The following information was presented on the reliability test:

Three members of the research staff participated in the reliability test. Five classes were selected at random from the complete list of 15 classes. From the five classes, two sessions were selected from each, yielding a total of 10 randomly selected class sessions. Randomly selected groups of moves from the beginning, the middle, and the end of the 10 class sessions were identified in order to establish a balanced sample of over 5 per cent of the 5,135 soliciting moves.

The three coders were divided into teams, one of which consisted of two coders and the other of a single coder. Assignment of coders to teams was rotated so that all possible permutations of pairs and singles were compared. Following the procedure for the coding of all other protocols, one member of the pair coded a given sample; the other member reviewed the coding; then both members of the pair arbitrated any disagreements. The single coder coded the sample and reviewed his own coding.

After each of the ten samples had been coded independently by the two teams, the codings were compared and the percentage of agreement among coders for each dimension was computed.[5]

[5] *Ibid.*, p. 104.

The results of the reliability estimates are shown in Table VI.

TABLE VI
Bellack's Per Cent of Agreement Among
Coding Teams in Content Analysis of
Soliciting Components

Category	Per Cent of Agreement
Total	97.1
Persons involved	96.4
Indicative meaning	99.0
Stylistic meaning	96.1

From Arno A. Bellack et al., *The Language of the Classroom*, p. 105.

As reported in the first study, the responding move accounts for 28.3 per cent of the moves in classroom discourse and 20.5 per cent of the lines. The chief function of the responding move is to satisfy the expectations of the soliciting move. Therefore, in a detailed analysis of the responding move, the concept of congruency was utilized, and the responding move was analyzed to discover how congruent it was with the soliciting move in terms of the following areas: Task Congruence, Logical Process Congruence, and Information Process Congruence.

The second initiatory move, the structuring move, accounts for only 5.5 per cent of the total pedagogical moves, but since the structuring move is generally longer than the other moves, its importance increases when one considers the percentage of lines devoted to structuring, 18.1 per cent.

In analyzing structuring in a detailed fashion, two concepts were used: (1) subgame, and (2) directive meaning. Just as Bellack speaks of the classroom game, he hypothesizes that subgames, such as debates, films, discussions, are played within the larger game and are set in motion by the structuring move. The directive meaning, as it applies to structuring, underscores the fact that the structuring move often serves to terminate one move and launch another. This function of structuring Bellack has termed the *halting-excluding* function.

The system for the analysis of the structuring move is presented below:

1. Function
   1.1 Launching
   1.2 Halting-excluding
2. Method
   2.1 Announcing

    2.2 Stating propositions
    2.3 Announcing and stating propositions
3. Activity
    3.1 General—oral
    3.2 Questioning-answering
    3.3 Reporting
    3.4 Debating
    3.5 Viewing/listening to audio-visual device
    3.6 Holding a panel discussion
    3.7 Following up a formal presentation
    3.8 Reading and/or reading and note taking
    3.9 Taking an examination
    3.10 Writing
    3.11 Voting
    3.12 Giving instructions
    3.13 Meeting in small groups
    3.14 Taking attendance
    3.15 Reviewing
    3.16 Taking a field trip
    3.17 Non-language routine
4. Agent
    4.1 Teachers and pupils
    4.2 All pupils
    4.3 Some pupils
    4.4 Pupil
    4.5 Teacher
    4.6 Teacher and pupil
    4.7 Teacher and some pupils
5. Topic
    5.1 Substantive
    5.2 Instructional
6. Logical process
7. Time
    7.1 Beginning point
      7.11 Present
      7.12 Future—this session
      7.13 Future—other session
      7.14 Future—unspecified
      7.15 Future—out of class
      7.16 Future—extra unit
    7.2 Duration
      7.21 Unit
      7.22 Sessions

    7.23 Session
    7.24 Segment
    7.25 Unspecified
  8. Regulation
  9. Instructional Aid
    9.1 Textbooks
    9.2 Charts, graphs, tables
    9.3 Maps, globes
    9.4 Books other than textbooks
    9.5 Films; recordings
    9.6 News media (newspaper, radio, television)
    9.7 Field trips
    9.8 Homework papers and assignments
    9.9 Classroom prepared material
  10. Reason[6]

The reliability of the analysis of the structuring move was obtained by using a method similar to that used to establish all the other reliability coefficients in the Bellack system. The reliability coefficients for the structuring move are reported in Table VII.

TABLE VII

Bellack's Per Cent of Agreement Among Coding Teams in the
Content Analysis of Structuring Components

Category	Per Cent of Agreement
Number of components in move	96.6
Function	100.0
Method	99.1
Activity announced	96.6
Agent announced	98.3
Duration of time	97.4
Beginning point in time	97.4
Substantive topic announced	94.1
Instructional topic announced	100.0
Logical process announced	92.3
Substantive and substantive-logical meanings stated	99.1
Reason giving	98.6
Regulations	89.8
Instructional aids	86.4

From Arno A. Bellack et al., *The Language of the Classroom*, p. 150.

While responding moves bear a reciprocal relation to soliciting, reacting moves may be occasioned by any of the four pedagogical moves. Reacting moves play a major role in classroom discourse,

[6] *Ibid.*, p. 138.

accounting for 30 per cent of the moves and 37.5 per cent of the lines. The pedagogical function of reaction moves is to ". . . *rate* (positively or negatively) and/or to *modify* (by clarifying, synthesizing or expanding) what was said in the moves that occasioned them."[7]

The system for the detailed analysis of the reacting move follows:

Reacting Move

1. *Reacting Move* (REA). Reacting is a reflexive pedagogical move that is occasioned by a structuring, soliciting, responding or another reacting move. Reactions are classified into three major categories: substantive, instructional, and substantive-instructional. Pedagogically, these moves serve to rate and/or to modify in some fashion what was stated in occasioning moves.

    Reacting moves differ from responding moves in that while a responding move is always directly elicited by a solicitation, preceding moves serve only as the occasion for reactions. For example, rating by a teacher of a pupil's response is designated a reacting move; that is, the student's response is the occasion for the teacher's rating reaction, but it does not actively elicit the reaction.

    1.1. Reacting (REA). A reaction to a single occasioning move.

    1.2. Reacting (REA). A reaction occasioned by more than one move.

    1.3. Reacting—Pause (REA*). The asterisk designates a reaction occasioned by a pause or by the absence of an expected responding move.

    1.4. Reacting—Physical (REA-P).

Types of Reacting Moves

1. *Substantive Reactions* are defined as (a) reactions that convey substantive meanings and associated substantive-logical meanings, and (b) reactions in the instructional and instructional-logical categories that are interpretations of preceding statements.

2. *Instructional Reactions* are defined as reactions that express instructional and associated instructional-logical meaning.

    2.1. *Rating Reactions*

        2.11. *Positive*

        2.12. *Admitting*

        2.13. *Repeating*

[7] *Ibid.*, p. 117.

2.14. *Qualifying*

2.15. *Not Admitting*

2.16. *Negative*

2.2. *Procedural Reactions* serve the pedagogical function of *modifying* by clarifying and/or expanding what has been said about procedural matters.

3. *Substantive-Instructional Reactions*

3.1. *Substantive-Rating Reactions*

3.2. *Substantive-Procedural Reactions*[8]

The observed patterning of classroom pedagogical moves led to the development of teaching cycles. The question whether cyclical patterns influence subsequent patterns was explored in Part II. Using the statistical method of Markov chain analysis, which offers a method of predicting the probability of moving from one state to another, this question was explored and some answers suggested.

TEACHER INFLUENCE, PUPIL ATTITUDES AND ACHIEVEMENT

As has already been noted, the observers who use Flanders' system write down a number at every three-second interval. The number is selected on the basis of the observer's estimate of how closely the observed classroom interaction approximates one of the ten categories of the Flanders category system. As the interaction progresses, numbers are written in a series. In order to facilitate later tabulations, the convention of beginning and ending each series with a ten, the category used to designate both noise and silence, was established.

A 10 X 10 matrix is used both to indicate in graphic form an interaction pattern and to tabulate the results. The numbers are tallied into a matrix by pairs; that is, the row selected represents the first number of the series, the column the second. Thus, each mark on the matrix represents two numbers of the series, and each number is recorded twice. Figure 1 shows an example of this kind of tabulation; a description of its use, given by Flanders, follows:

> The numbers are tallied in the matrix one pair at a time. The column is used for the second number, the row is used for the first number. The first pair is 10-6: the tally is placed in the row ten column six cell. The second pair is 6-10: tally this in the row six column ten cell. The third pair is 10-7, the fourth pair is 7-5, and so on. Each pair overlaps with the next and the total number of observations, "N," always will be tabulated by N-1 tallies in the matrix. In this case we

[8] Arno A. Bellack et al., *The Language of the Classroom*, p. 172.

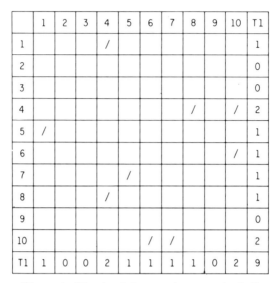

	1	2	3	4	5	6	7	8	9	10	T1
1				/							1
2											0
3											0
4							/		/		2
5	/										1
6									/		1
7					/						1
8				/							1
9											0
10						/	/				2
T1	1	0	0	2	1	1	1	1	0	2	9

Figure 1. Flanders' interaction matrix indicating example of scoring technique. (From Ned A. Flanders, "Teacher Influence, Pupil Attitudes, and Achievement," Appendix F, p. 16.)

started a series of ten numbers and the series produced nine tallies in the matrix.[9]

The observer is instructed to record numbers in a series until there is a major change in class formation, communication pattern, or subject matter. When a change occurs, the observer is instructed to draw a double line to indicate the ending of one series and the beginning of a new one. A matrix might include the tabulations of a single tabulated series or a group of tabulated series. Matrices may be combined to form a single matrix that indicates the results of many hours of observations, or of many different classes or of many different teachers.

The matrix shown in Figure 2 indicates, by letter, those places where information is tallied. The tallied information makes possible multiple interpretations. Those columns grouped under the letter A, when totaled, represent the amount of time the teacher talks; the two columns subsumed under the B category, when totaled, indicate the amount of student talk, and the C column represents the amount of either silence or confusion in any one complete tallied period. The columns of teacher talk grouped under the letter A can be divided

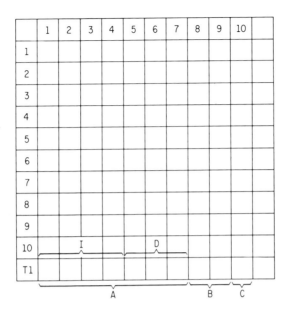

Figure 2. Flanders' interaction matrix indicating total tally cells. (From Ned A. Flanders, "Teacher Influence, Pupil Attitudes, and Achievement," p. 36.)

into those columns that represent indirect influence, columns 1, 2, 3, 4, and those columns that represent direct influence, 5, 6, 7.

Where desired, an indirect-direct ratio can be calculated by placing the combined totals of columns 1, 2, 3, 4 above the combined totals of columns 5, 6, 7. This is called the i/d ratio. Sometimes the i/d ratio is computed without the 4 and 5 column totals, which are the question asking categories. It is stated in the study that the removal of categories 4 and 5, which are subject-matter influenced columns, in computing the i/d ratio gives a clearer picture of teacher influence patterns.

Figure 3 indicates the "steady state" cells. These cells are along the diagonal from the upper left to the lower right. Markings in any one of these cells occur when a speaker is observed to be using the same category for more than three seconds at a time.

In Figure 4 the shaded area A indicates positive teacher-student interaction, since the charted shift is from praise to the clarification and development of student ideas or the shift is in the reverse direction. Marks in this area also indicate the teacher's concern with positive motivation and reward. The shaded area B is called the "vicious circle" by Flanders, in that it indicates the shift from teacher giving directions to student resisting, to teacher criticism, to further student resistance, and the like.

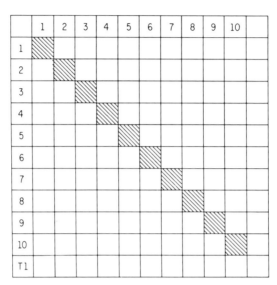

Figure 3. Flanders' interaction matrix indicating "steady state" cells. (From Ned A. Flanders, "Teacher Influence, Pupil Attitudes, and Achievement," p. 37.)

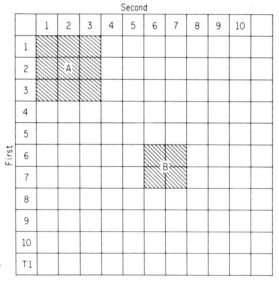

Figure 4. Flanders' interaction matrix indicating both positive and negative teacher-student interaction areas. (From Ned A. Flanders, "Teacher Influence, Pupil Attitudes, and Achievement," p. 38.)

What Flanders refers to as the content cross is indicated in Figure 5. Tallies in the shaded area indicate that questions are being asked and information given.

Second

	1	2	3	4	5	6	7	8	9	10	
1			/	//	//	/					
2			/	//	//	/					
3	/	/	/	//	//	/	/	/	/	/	
4	//	//	//	//	//	//	//	//	//	//	
5	//	//	//	//	//	//	//	//	//	//	
6	/	/	/	//	//	/	/	/	/	/	
7			/	//	//	/					
8			/	//	//	/					
9			/	//	//	/					
10			/	//	//	/					
T1			/	//	//	/					

First

Figure 5. Flanders' interaction matrix indicating "content cross." (From Ned A. Flanders, "Teacher Influence, Pupil Attitudes, and Achievement," p. 39.)

Since the decisions crucial to the use of the Flanders study are those made by the coders in the classroom, the question of reliability will be discussed as it applies to classroom coder reliability. Flanders reports the following information about coder reliability:

> Training of both old and new observers took place prior to the teaching of the first unit of study. During the first part of this training the new members of the team achieved Scott reliability ratings which ranged from 0.64 to 9.76. With additional training these ratings improved until the between-observer Scott reliabilities were consistently above 0.85.
>
> Throughout the data collecting period the observers met together about once a week. At these meetings any unusual classification problems were discussed and a policy established so that if other observers faced the same problem later on they could react consistently. [10]

Medley and Mitzel, in their review of the Flanders study, discussed the question of coder reliability and the uses that Flanders had made of his reliability scores. They make the point that Flanders' coefficients of observer agreement were calculated only for the combined area totals A, B, C, and were calculated on the basis of one visit of unspecified length. Since some of the classroom visits were one hour, and others of two-hour duration, Medley and Mitzel

[10] Ned A. Flanders, "Teacher Influence, Pupil Attitudes, and Achievement," p. 72.

appear to indicate that different time span, if taken into account, might have in some fashion altered the results:

> For the uses of the technique suggested by Flanders these reliabilities have limited relevance . . . .
>
> Use of the score either for comparing different teachers or for studying differences in a single teacher's behavior in these different types of situations implies inferences about unobserved behavior, particularly when behaviors are related to student achievement, attitudes, "dependence proneness," and the like. Satisfactory evidence of reliability of the records and scores based on them would have to show that teacher behavior (within a given type of situation) is stable enough in relation to observed differences between teachers to warrant such inferences.
>
> . . . A critical ratio justifying rejection of the null hypothesis is *de facto* evidence that the measuring instrument used had reliability sufficient for the purpose for which it was used.[11]

Within the Flanders second year study, another system of analysis was used. The purpose of this second analysis was to classify teacher behavior so as to have a basis for judging a teacher's flexibility:

> The concept of teacher flexibility was operationally defined in terms of the question, does the teacher adapt his pattern of influence to the different types of classroom activities? Our observers were able to classify classroom episodes into 36 separate activities. It was decided to arrange the activities into four categories of planning, work, evaluation, and administration. Each observer presented his original notes about the activity period at a staff meeting of all observers, explained the conditions present at the time, and then proposed a classification of the episode into one of the four categories. After full discussion, the group decision was considered final.
>
> Some of the activities were considered to have greater potential for student participation and expression of opinion. For example, a teacher can give an assignment that will have an unknown effect on subsequent student participation or expression of opinion, but the process of giving the assignment *per se* is likely to be restricting. Teacher-pupil planning of an assignment, on the other hand, involves a process that provides for student expression of opinion. It was decided to classify some of the planning and work activities according to whether they possessed greater potential for stimulating student participation and expression of opinion and to classify others that possessed less potential. The former were called "expanding" and labeled "E"; the latter were called "restricting" and labeled "R." Only the more obvious classifications were made. The entire list of the 36 activities, their classification into four major activity categories, and their assignment to the "E" or "R" category can be found on the next page.[12]

[11] Donald Medley and Harold E. Mitzel, "Measuring Classroom Behavior by Systematic Observation," in N. L. Gage, ed., American Educational Research Association *Handbook of Research on Teaching* (Chicago: Rand McNally, 1963), pp. 273, 274.

[12] Ned A. Flanders, "Teacher Influence, Pupil Attitudes, and Achievement," p. 75.

It is important to note here that an episode, the crucial unit in judging teacher flexibility, was defined operationally as a series of numbered interactions beginning with the ten designation and continuing until a major change in class formation, communication, or subject matter occurred. As that change occurred, the coder would add a ten to the series, draw a double line, and the episode would thus be all the interactions between the double line. Although the episode is the unit of analysis for judging teacher flexibility, no reliability tests or measures are presented for the episode in Flanders' study. Taba and Smith both state in their studies the difficulty of agreeing on the beginning and ending of their basic units of analysis, the "thought unit" in Taba's case, the "venture" in Smith's. These facts lead to the observation that some evidence of the reliability of the episode as a measure in the Flanders study would have been helpful in evaluating Flanders' findings on teacher flexibility.

FLANDERS' CATEGORIES FOR CLASSROOM ACTIVITIES

Evaluative Category:

A. PLANNING

R*	1.	Long-range planning, teacher assigns and describes work
E**	2.	Long-range teacher-pupil planning
R	3.	Immediate goal, teacher assigns work
E	4.	Immediate goal, teacher-pupil planning

B. WORK

Teacher-Directed

R	5.	Teacher gives directions for current activities
R	6.	Teacher lectures
R	7.	Teacher reads to class
	8.	Listening to outside speaker
	9.	Listening to tapes or records
	10.	Viewing slides, films, pictures
R	11.	Oral reading, by turns
R	12.	Prepared oral reading
R	13.	Drill
R	14.	Recitation (teacher questions, pupils answer)
E	15.	Teacher answers pupils' questions
E	16.	Teacher led discussion or blackboard work

*Participation restricted.
**Participation expanded.

Pupil-Directed

E   17. Silent reading of pupil-selected material
    18. Silent reading of assigned material
    19. Individual seat work or blackboard work
E   20. Subgroups and individual seat work
E   21. Subgroups working
E   22. Pupil-led discussion

C. EVALUATION

Teacher-Directed

    23. Test
    24. Correcting papers or homework
    25. Teacher-led discussion

Pupil-Directed

    26. Individual reports
    27. Group reports
    28. Pupil led discussion

D. ADMINISTRATIVE MATTERS AND NON-UNIT ROUTINE PROCEDURES

    29. Pencil sharpening
    30. Settling down (wasted time)
    31. Clean up
    32. Necessary routine; return papers, record grades
    33. Administrative details
    34. Break
    35. Non-unit activities
    36. Games (this activity was found in only one class)[13]

ASSESSMENT OF THE QUALITY OF TEACHING

Stenographic records provided the basis for the Hughes analysis of classroom interaction. The unit identified in the Hughes study for categorization is the *function*, and each function is categorized as an act of the teacher's. In making decisions concerning the categorization of a particular function, the following question was asked: "What function did this verbal behavior and/or non-verbal behavior perform for a child, group, or class?"[14] It was seen that a *function* as

[13] *Ibid.,* p. 89.
[14] Marie M. Hughes and Associates, "The Assessment of the Quality of Teaching: A Research Report," U.S. Office of Education Cooperative Research Project No. 353 (Salt Lake City: University of Utah, 1959), p. 41.

a unit was not congruent with any grammatical division and had to be determined within the teaching context. The following information summarizes the decisions made concerning the identification of functions:

Function is identified and counted only for teacher-learner interaction that is in *direct focus.*

More than one function may be assigned a given unit of verbal and/or non-verbal behavior when it is recognized as performing a function of equal potency for two different children or groups. Under these conditions more than one child or group is in direct focus in the teacher-learner interaction. [15]

The code by which Hughes analyzed classroom interaction contains thirty-one functions subsumed under seven categories. Each of the listed functions has a subscript which describes the manner in which these functions can be performed. The code is outlined below.

OUTLINE OF THE UNIVERSITY OF UTAH REVISION OF THE PROVO CODE FOR THE ANALYSIS OF TEACHING

Controlling Functions

Structure	Regulate
open	open
closed	closed
intervention	global
sequential	routine
orientation	neutral
ongoing	sequential
public criteria	direction
	public criteria
Standard Set	Judge
recall	direction
teacher edict	punish
group developed	turn back
universal	just

Imposition of Teacher

Regulate Self	Inform Appraisal
Moralize	Inform
Teacher Estimate of Need	

Facilitating Functions

Checking	Demonstrate
information	Clarify Procedure
routine	
involvement	

[15]*Ibid.,* p. 49.

Functions That Develop Content

Resource
  routine
  child initiative
Stimulate
  one
  three
Structure, Turn Back
Content-Agree

Clarify
  just
  content
  generalize
  summarize
Evaluate
  just
  negative
  positive
  with discrimination

Functions That Serve as Response

Meets Request
  routine
  makes arrangements
Clarify Personal
  problem
  experience

Interprets
  situation
  feelings
Acknowledges Teacher
Mistake

Functions of Positive Affectivity

Support
  just
  stereotype
  specific

Solicitous
Encourage
Does for Personal

Functions of Negative Affectivity

Admonish
Reprimand
  public criteria
Accusative
Threat

Negative Response Personal
  public criteria
Verbal Futuristic
  public criteria
Ignore[16]

Hughes describes the steps taken to ensure coder reliability:

The 105 records were coded by the four members of the research staff who worked in pairs, each coding the record individually, then coming together with a checker to work through the disagreements in their coding. With one exception, no teacher had a record coded until a record from all others had been coded. Only a few teachers had a second record coded by the same team.

The 105 records totaled 1125½ pages of type-written material. The individual records ranged from seven to fifteen and a half pages, with a median of 10½ pages per record. Twenty per cent of the pages were recoded to provide the index of percentage of agreement. The pages

16 *Ibid.*, p. 60.

were selected by formula so that each record contributed according to its total number of pages. The recoding was done by the original pair and the same process of working through a checker continued.

The recoding does not represent precisely the same situation because the pages were taken at random, thus appeared out of context; however, the full typed record was available for reference. A complete cycle of records was coded before the recoding on the previous cycle was done. The percentage of agreement between the two codings is based on an item by item analysis.

On the 1125½ pages, 2345 were recoded with percentage agreement of 81.4. When the data are corrected for agreement within categories, the percentage-agreement becomes 83.6 [Table VIII].

TABLE VIII
Hughes' Overall Percentage-Agreement on Recording

Total Acts	Total Acts Recoded	Total Acts Disagree	Total Acts Agree	Per Cent of Agreement
26,385	5,467	1,017	4,450	81.4
Corrected for within category agreement	5,467	894	4,573	83.6

From Marie M. Hughes and Associates, "The Assessment of the Quality of Teaching," p. 81.

Table IX represents Hughes' percentage of agreement according to category. Percentages were tabulated to ascertain the patterns of teacher functions. By means of a graph Hughes indicated the pattern of teaching she would consider to be good in its percentage distribution of functions. Hughes then indicated on a graph and on a table those six thirty-minute specimen teaching records that came closest to her proposed model. Figure 6 is the graphic presentation of these records, followed by Table X containing this same information.

TABLE IX
Hughes' Percentage-Agreement on Recoding According to Category

Category	Total Items Recoded	Inter- and Intra-Category Agreements	Inter-Category Disagreements and Omissions	Percentage of Agreement
Controlling	2,527	2,219	308	87.8
Imposition	174	109	65	62.6
Facilitating	414	298	116	71.9
Content development	886	751	135	84.7
Response	277	208	69	75.1
Positive affectivity	612	519	93	84.8
Negative affectivity	577	469	108	81.2
Total	5,467	4,573	894	83.6

From Marie M. Hughes and Associates, "The Assessment of the Quality of Teaching," p. 84.

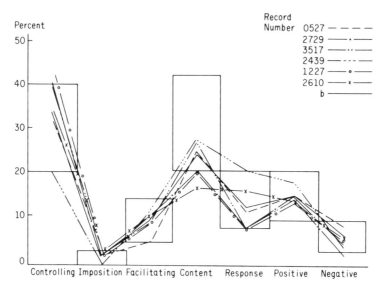

Figure 6. Hughes' distribution of teaching acts for six thirty-minute teaching records considered to be nearest to the model—in graphic form. (From Marie M. Hughes and Associates, "The Assessment of the Quality of Teaching," p. 225.) (*b*, The solid line indicates the mean of the six thirty-minute records considered to be nearest the model.)

Analyses of variance were performed on the data to determine the answers to the following questions:

1. Is there a difference between the judged-good teachers from fourteen different schools and the ten representative teachers who came from one school?
2. Is there a difference between primary teachers as a group and intermediate teachers as a group?

TABLE X

Hughes' Distribution of Teaching Acts for Six Thirty-Minute Teaching
Records Considered to be Nearest to the Model

Record Number	Total Acts	Controlling		Imposition		Facilitating		Content		Response		Positive		Negative	
		No.	%	No.	%	No.	%	No.	%	No.	%	No.	%	No.	%
0527	168	54	32	5	3	9	5	41	24	20	12	25	15	14	9
2729	338	134	40	8	2	37	11	66	20	28	8	50	15	15	4
3517	195	76	39	6	3	16	8	50	26	16	8	27	14	4	2
2439	208	41	20	2	1	23	11	55	26	41	20	37	18	9	4
1227	224	91	42	5	2	23	10	46	20	19	8	29	13	11	5
2610	221	77	35	7	3	21	10	37	17	36	16	32	14	11	5
*			35		2		9		22		12		15		5

*Indicates the mean of the six thirty-minute records considered to be nearest the model.

From Marie M. Hughes and Associates, "The Assessment of the Quality of Teaching," p. 226.

3. Is there a difference when teaching is examined according to content?
4. Is there a difference among teachers when they are grouped according to deviations from the model of *good teaching*?
5. Is there a difference between teachers on each of the seven major categories?

The intercorrelations of categories were examined to determine what different correlations existed between different content situations.

THE LOGIC OF TEACHING

In the first Smith study the central unit of analysis was the episode. The episode was described as: "A unit of discourse involving a verbal exchange between at least two individuals. It passes typically through three phases: (a) an initial or opening phase, (b) a sustained or continuing phase, and (c) a terminal or closing phase."[17]

The first phase of an episode, the entry, is described as follows: "The initial or opening phase of an episode always contains a remark or set of remarks (assertions, questions, announcements, etc.) which is called an entry."[18] The continuing phase of an episode is composed of remarks that are: (a) either replies or responses to a question, (b) claims, comments, or opinions, (c) questions that sustain the entry or point under discussion, and (d) anomalous questions. An episode may pass through an overtly terminal phase or be closed off by the abrupt change of topic or subject which signals the opening of a new episode.

After identifying the three phases of the episode, Smith classified episodes by their entries or opening phases into the following categories, and entitled his classification:

CRITERIA FOR CLASSIFYING ENTRIES

1. Defining (contains four subcategories)
2. Describing (containing 22 subcategories)
3. Designating (containing 5 subcategories)
4. Stating (containing 5 subcategories)
5. Reporting (containing 3 subcategories)
6. Substituting (containing 2 subcategories)
7. Evaluating (containing 4 subcategories)
8. Opining (containing 6 subcategories)
9. Classifying (containing 1 subcategory)

[17]B. Othanel Smith and Milton O. Meux, "A Study of the Logic of Teaching" (Urbana: Bureau of Educational Research, College of Education, University of Illinois, 1963), p. 21.

[18]*Ibid.*, p. 21.

10. Comparing and Contrasting (containing 4 subcategories)
11. Conditional Inferring (containing 8 subcategories)
12. Explaining
    12.1 Mechanical Explaining (with 2 subcategories)
    12.2 Causal Explaining (with 5 subcategories)
    12.3 Sequent Explaining (with 4 subcategories)
    12.4 Procedural Explaining (with 4 subcategories)
    12.5 Teleological Explaining (with 5 subcategories)
    12.6 Normative Explaining (with 5 subcategories)
13. Directing and Managing Classroom (containing 5 subcategories)

Reliability in the Smith study for the episode and monologue, the units of analysis, and for the classification of the units was estimated after the criteria were established. Smith discusses the question of reliability, first as it centers on the estimate of the number of units for analysis in the transcripts:

> The first step in the final testing consisted in each of the four judges marking off independently what he judged to be the total set of units (both episodes and monologs) on each transcript. He numbered each utterance with the number of the criterion he thought it satisfied. The judges were instructed to distinguish the greatest number of units which could result from applying the criteria.
>
> In the second step of the final testing, the four judges worked in two teams of two judges each. Within each team, the two judges together considered each utterance in the light of the criteria and their original assessments of each utterance. After this step, many disagreements were eliminated; others persisted.

Listed below are the coefficients of agreement on number of units, episodes, and monologues that were obtained in selected tapes from U.S. History and English.

Tape Number and Subject	Coefficient
1. U.S. History	.71
2. U.S. History	.73
3. U.S. History	.62
4. English	.71
5. English	.70
6. English	.64
7. English	.69

The coefficients range from .62 to .73—a fairly small range—with a median of .70.[21]

A system similar to the one used for obtaining estimates of reliability for the identification of units of analysis was used to estimate the reliability of the criteria. Smith describes the training of the judges and reports the results:

[19] *Ibid.*, Appendix 3, p. 211.
[20] *Ibid.*, p. 20.
[21] *Ibid.*, p. 28.

Two sample sets of entries were used for the purpose of training the judges. The first was an easy set containing about 55 entries. The other set was more difficult and contained about 120 entries.

After classifying the first set of easy entries independently of each other, the judges met with the staff to check their agreement and to discuss difficulties encountered. The judges then classified the second set of more difficult entries and afterwards met again to check their agreement and to discuss difficulties they encountered.

The final set of about 300 entries was then classified by the judges. The entries in this final set were selected randomly from the entries already classified by the staff. In all but three of the categories— Defining, Explaining, and Designating—one out of four entries were selected randomly. In each of the subcategories of Defining and Explaining, one out of three entries were selected randomly, and in the subcategories of Designating one out of four entries were selected randomly. The one exception was Substituting, which had so few entries that they were all used in the final set.

The agreement on this final set of entries was determined for two pairs of judges. This latter procedure was used to minimize the number of sheer oversights likely to occur—rather than actual misjudgments and misapplications of the criteria. Thus, these coefficients are for pairs of judges, not single judges.

The formula for calculating the coefficient was based upon the number of agreements per category between the two pairs of judges. Thus each category has a separate coefficient.[22]

The coefficient of agreement that Smith obtains is reported in Table XI:

TABLE XI
Smith's Coefficients of Agreement for the Criteria for the Logical Categories

Name of Category	Coefficient	Name of Category	Coefficient
Defining		Evaluating	.60
(1)	.88	Opining	.73
(2)	.88	Classifying	.70
(3)	.33	Comparing and	
(4)	0.00	contrasting	.62
T[a]	.84	Conditional	
Describing	.67	inferring	.67
Designating		Explaining	
(1)	.64	(1)	.83
(2)	.62	(2)	.55
(3)	.48	(3)	.36
(4)	.90	(4)	.67
(5)	1.00	(5)	.67
T	.71	(6)	.76
Stating	.63	T	.84
Reporting	.33	Directing and	
Substituting	.88	managing classroom	.87

From B. Othanel Smith and Milton O. Meux, "A Study of the Logic of Teaching," p. 45.
[a]The entries designated T—under Defining, Designating, and Explaining—are for these categories as a whole.

[22]*Ibid.*, p. 44.

As can be seen [in Table XI], the coefficients range from 0.00 to 1.00. The median is .67, and the middle 50 per cent of the coefficients range from .62 to .84—a fairly high percentage of agreement for the present status of the categories.[23]

Smith tabulated his logical categories both by subject and area and by area alone. The tabulation just by area is shown in Table XII.

TABLE XII

Smith's Distribution of Logical Categories by Areas

Category	Area					Number of Entries in the Category	Percent of Total Number of Entries
	Math.	Sci.	S.S.	Eng.	Core		
1. Defining							
1.11	5	23	20	21	0	66	2.0
1.12	4	21	12	7	0	44	1.3
1.13	0	0	6	4	0	10	0.3
1.14	0	13	1	1	1	16	0.5
1T	9	57	39	33	1	139	4.1
2. Describing	97	294	218	175	77	861	25.3
3. Designating							
3.11	1	36	17	17	0	71	2.1
3.12	4	15	7	8	0	34	1.0
3.13	29	73	21	55	14	192	5.7
3.14	0	14	106	26	4	150	4.4
3.15	2	21	12	19	3	57	1.7
3T	36	159	163	125	21	504	14.8
4. Stating	58	29	36	103	4	230	6.8
5. Reporting	6	30	33	12	18	99	2.9
6. Substituting	4	4	2	0	0	10	0.3
7. Evaluating	2	22	53	70	9	156	4.6
8. Opining	6	21	89	51	12	179	5.3
9. Classifying	11	30	11	44	7	103	3.0
10. Comparing and contrasting	11	43	27	29	2	112	3.3
11. Conditional inferring	37	82	64	50	15	248	7.3
12. Explaining							
12.1 Mechanical	0	19	0	1	1	21	0.6
12.2 Causal	0	39	49	23	3	114	3.4
12.3 Sequent	16	5	32	12	0	49	1.4
12.4 Procedural	2	21	9	11	5	62	1.8
12.5 Teleological	22	11	30	31	5	79	2.3
12.6 Normative	40	18	16	56	1	113	3.3
12T	39	113	136	134	15	438	12.9
13. Directing and managing classroom	0	50	102	78	49	318	9.4
Total number of entries in area	356	934	973	904	230	3,397	

From B. Othanel Smith and Milton O. Meux, "A Study of the Logic of Teaching," p. 54.

[23] *Ibid.*, p. 45.

Smith's second study dealt with the analysis of a unit of instruction called a venture: "A venture is a segment of discourse consisting of a set of utterances dealing with a single topic and having a single overarching content objective.[24] Smith details the criteria for identifying a venture in the following fashion:

> 1. The beginning of a venture is identified by one or more of the following:
> 1.1. An utterance or part of an utterance containing an explicit indication (announcement or proposal), usually by the teacher, that a particular topic is to be considered.
> 1.2. An utterance containing a question or statement that makes a marked change in the course of the discussion.
> 1.3 An utterance containing a question or statement that initiates a discussion characterized by a new overarching objective.[25]

After testing the exceptions and qualifications to this identification, Smith describes his process of securing coder reliability on the identification of venture:

> At the end of the training period each judge was given nine tape transcripts in which he was to identify ventures. These nine tapes represented a variety of different subject matters and grade levels. When the judges had marked their tape transcripts individually, they were divided into two teams having two members each. Each team then arrived at a team judgment of the ventures occurring in each tape transcript. The team judgments were used as the basis for calculating the coefficient of interjudge agreement for each tape.[26]

Smith's coefficients of agreement between judges are shown in Table XIII.

TABLE XIII

Smith's Coefficients of Agreement between Judges

Subject	Grade	Coefficient of Agreement
World History	10	.86
World History	10	.89
United States History	11	.58
Sociology	11–12	.87
English	11	.70
English	9	.60
Physiology	10–11	.56
Physics	11	.67
Geometry	10	.75

From B. Othanel Smith and Milton O. Meux, "A Tentative Report on Strategies of Teaching," p. 17.

[24] B. Othanel Smith and Milton O. Meux, "A Tentative Report on Strategies of Teaching," U.S. Office of Education, Department of Health, Education, and Welfare, Project No. 1640 (Urbana: Bureau of Educational Research, College of Education, University of Illinois, 1964), p. 5.

[25] *Ibid.*, p. 12.

[26] *Ibid.*, p. 50.

In continuing the discussion of ventures, Smith described the venture as having a control point: "There is a sort of conclusion to which the verbal exchanges lead, a sort of theme that seems to pervade the exchanges. This constitutes the import of the venture, and it is its import that we have in mind when we speak of the venture's objective."[27] Ventures were then categorized by their content objectives and identified as being one of nine different types:

    1. *Causal Venture.* identification, description, or discussion of events, agents, or characteristics which are said to cause, generate, or facilitate the occurence of a particular phenomenon or class of phenomena.

    2. *Conceptual Venture.* discloses the condition or criteria governing the use of a term.

    3. *Evaluative Venture.* decides whether X is good or bad, right or wrong, fair or unfair, etc.

    4. *Informatory Venture.* provides information or evidence to clarify or amplify a specified topic or group of related topics.

    5. *Interpretive Venture.* discloses the meaning or significance of a set of words or symbols or a bit of discourse.

    6. *Procedural Venture.* describes how to perform an activity, reach a solution, carry through a plan, etc.

    7. *Reason Venture.* identifies or discusses the reasons for an action, event, or conclusion.

    8. *Rule Venture.* used when making decisions based on rules.

    9. *System Venture.* used for the functional interrelationships of the parts of some unit that operates to produce or secure a given end.[28]

Two teams of judges were used to estimate the reliability of identifying these nine ventures. The proportions of agreement between teams

TABLE XIV
Smith's Proportions of Agreement between Teams
in the Use of Each Category

Type of Venture Agreed upon	Coefficients of Agreement
1. Causal	.00[a]
2. Reason	.67
3. Conceptual	.75
4. Evaluative	.75
5. Informatory	.75
6. Interpretive	.67
7. Procedural	.80
8. Rule	.86
9. System	1.00

    From B. Othanel Smith and Milton O. Meux, "A Tentative Report on Strategies of Teaching," p. 43.
    [a]When the Causal and Reason categories—which are not customarily distinguished in the language and are thus easily confused by naive judges—are combined, the proportion of agreement for the combined categories is .80.

[27]*Ibid.*, p. 221.
[28]*Ibid.*, p. 99.

in the use of each category is shown in Table XIV. Except for the Causal category, the proportions of agreement range from .67 (Evaluative category) to 1.00 (System category), with a median of .75.

Following Smith's classification of venture, he moves to a description and definition of his concept of strategy: "Pedagogically, strategy refers to a set of verbal actions that serves to attain certain results and to guard against others."[29] Smith suggests that strategy has two dimensions: the treatment dimension and the control dimension. The treatment dimension concerns: "The type and sequence of operations that the teacher and the students jointly enter into in setting forth and structuring information in such a way as to disclose the content that has to be learned."[30] The control dimension ". . . has to do with the operations the teacher uses to guide and control the participation of students in performing these operations on the content."[31]

Smith concentrates the remainder of his study on the treatment dimension of strategy. He states that to describe the treatment dimension of a strategy, one must identify the kinds of verbal manipulations of the content of instruction. These verbal manipulations Smith identifies as moves. A move, as identified by him, is ". . . a verbal activity which logically or analytically relates terms of the proposition set forth by the strategy to some event or thing or to some class of events or things."[32]

Moves always carry content. Ten kinds of content which moves carry were identified by Smith as:

1. A part the referent has.
2. A characteristic of the referent.
3. A function of the referent.
4. A characteristic use of the referent.
5. A characteristic treatment accorded the referent.
6. A physical relationship between the referent and something else.
7. The way in which the referent compares to something else with respect to a particular characteristic.
8. The evaluative rating implied by the use of the term.
9. A condition necessary or required to produce or cause the referent.
10. The results of an operation involving the referent.[33]

Smith analyzed ventures into moves; however, although he had

[29]*Ibid.*, p. 50.
[30]*Ibid.*, p. 51.
[31]*Ibid.*
[32]*Ibid.*, p. 54.
[33]*Ibid.*, p. 55.

identified nine kinds of ventures, only conceptual ventures were analyzed into moves. It was suggested that there are eighteen kinds of moves: criterion description, analysis, enumeration, classification, classificatory description, analogy, differentiation, negation, opposition, sufficient condition, instance production, positive instance, negative instance, instance substantiation, instance comparison, instance variance, operation variance, and meta distinction.

After enumerating and identifying eighteen different moves that characterize the conceptual ventures, Smith suggests that strategies are composed of combinations of moves. However, he does assert that it is possible to identify a certain type of strategy as containing only one move.

Tentatively, Smith identifies four kinds of strategy: Type I strategy, which contains four subtypes; Type II; Type III; and Type IV strategy.

> *Sub-type A*—These are strategies which contain only one move.[34]
> *Sub-type B*—A strategy of this type contains an initial abstract move (other than a criterion description move) supplemented by one or more criterion description moves.[35]
> *Sub-type C*—This strategy is one which begins with a criterion move and culminates with a different type of abstract move.[36]
> *Sub-type D*—Strategies of this type contain both criterion description moves and other abstract moves.[37]

In Type II strategies, as designed by Smith, one or more abstract moves are followed by one or more instancing moves. The Type III strategy is a reverse of the Type II pattern in that one or more instancing moves precede one or more abstracting moves. The fourth type of strategy is identified as a mixed move containing both instancing and abstracting moves. Although reliability coefficients are reported for both the identification and classification of ventures, Smith does not report how classroom discourse, as derived from his tapescripts, was divided into ventures, moves, or strategies. Also, no reliability was reported for the identification of a move as a unit for analysis, the identification of a particular kind of move in terms of the eighteen class category for conceptual ventures, the identification of a strategy as a unit of analysis, or the identification of a strategy as belonging to either one of four types or as belonging to one of four types and one of the four subtypes within Type I.

[34]*Ibid.*, p. 61
[35]*Ibid.*, p. 64
[36]*Ibid.*, p. 68.
[37]*Ibid.*, p. 72.

THINKING IN ELEMENTARY SCHOOL CHILDREN

Taba describes her coding scheme as based on a multidimensional analysis of classroom interaction. She lists the requirements that her analysis system had to satisfy:

1. The coding of teacher behavior in terms of the pedagogical functions this behavior serves in the development of cognitive processes of the students.
2. Categorizing students' responses in a manner which describes (a) the nature of their cognitive operations, and (b) yields a direct measure of the quality of these operations, and in terms of their complexity and abstractness.
3. A way of relating teaching strategies to the cognitive behavior they produce in students. [38]

Taba's unit for analysis, the "thought unit," was defined as ". . . a remark or series of remarks which expresses a more or less complete idea, serves a specified function, and can be classified by a level of thought." [39]

Verbal transactions were coded on three dimensions; the first designation describes the *source* of the thought unit. There are four such possible designations:

> (CG) child gives
> (CS) child seeks
> (TG) teacher gives
> (TS) teacher seeks

The second designation is *function*. Two different groups of functions were identified. One group serves a psychological or managerial function and is coded:

> (A) agreement
> (AP) approval
> (D) disagreement
> (DP) disapproval
> (M) management
> (R) reiteration

The second group, which *functions* to direct discussion and can be related both to level of thought and the logic of the content, includes:

[38] Hilda Taba and others, "Thinking in Elementary School Children," U.S. Department of Health, Education, and Welfare, Cooperative Research Program, Project No. 1574 (San Francisco: San Francisco State College, 1964), p. 114.
[39] *Ibid.*, p. 115.

(F)   focusing
(FR)   refocusing
(FC)   change of focus
(C)   controlling thought
(X)   extending thought on
      the same level
(L)   lifting thought to
      a higher level

As to the third coding, *level of thought*, this dimension, states Taba:

> ... describes both the student's and the teacher's verbal behavior by specifying the logical quality and the level of thought expressed. A separate coding scheme was developed for each of the three cognitive tasks, and categories were established to represent hierarchical levels of thought, such as giving information (10, 11, 12), grouping (30, 31, 32), and categorizing (40, 41, 42) in the cognitive task of grouping and labeling. These categories refer to specific thought processes which need to be mastered in a sequential order, because the mastery on the preceding level is a prerequisite to performance on the next. Thus, this coding scheme in a sense represents the developmental sequence of steps for each cognitive task. In addition within each category, distinctions were made between the irrelevant, the disconnected, and the contextual or related information. Thus, where possible, the distinctions within a category were ordered from lower to high levels of thought.[40]

Thus, the coding systems for identifying levels of thought are hierarchical in character. They are presented below:

> *The thought level codings.* These codings identify the level of thought contained in the thought unit. Within each thought level there are three codings: in the units place of the code the zero (0) code indicates a thought unit that is irrelevant or incorrect; the one (1) code indicates a correct response at that thought level without elaboration; the two (2) code indicates a correct response at that thought level which is accompanied by some qualifying or explanatory statements.
>
> The coding scheme for the cognitive task of predicting consequences contains an additional code in the units place for prediction. This three (3) code is used to designate a prediction accompanied by a stated or implied principle.

Cognitive task: Grouping and labeling (giving or seeking)

10   specific or general information outside of focus
11   specific or general information within focus
12   specific or general information with qualifications

30   grouping information without basis
31   grouping information with implicit basis
32   grouping information with explicit basis

---

[40] *Ibid.*, p. 117.

40 categorizing information without basis
41 categorizing information with implicit relationships between items
42 categorizing information with explicit relationships between them

Cognitive task: interpreting information and making inferences (giving or seeking)

10 specific or general information outside of focus
11 specific or general information within focus
12 specific or general information with qualifications and relationships
50 specific reason or explanation that does not relate to the information
51 specific reason or explanation that relates or organizes the information
52 specific reason or explanation that states how it relates or organizes the information

60 irrelevant or incorrect inference which is derived from information
61 relevant inference which is derived from information
62 relevant inference which is derived from information and expresses a cause and effect relationship, explanation, consequence, or contrast

70 relationship between information which implies an irrelevant or incorrect principle or generalization
71 relationship between information which implies a principle or generalization
72 principle or generalization which is derived from information

Cognitive task: predicting consequences (giving or seeking)

90 correcting the cause or condition

Establishing parameters of information

100 relevant information
101 relevant information for establishing the parameter for a particular hypothesis or prediction
102 relevant information for the parameter or any particular prediction with appropriate explanation

Establishing parameters of conditions

110 irrelevant or untenable condition for the logical parameter (if-then) or for the particular prediction or hypothesis
111 relevant condition without connecting it with relevant information
112 relevant condition and information and establishing logical connection between them

Prediction: Level one (100), immediate consequences
        Level two (200), remote consequences

120-220 incorrect or out of focus prediction
121-221 prediction with no elaboration
122-222 prediction accompanied by explanation, qualification, differentiation, comparison, or contrast
123-223 prediction accompanied by a stated or implied principle
        To determine the statement coding, each thought unit is first

judged and coded according to its level of thought (whether in the 10's, 40's, 60's, etc.) and then is coded as 0, 1, or 2, depending upon the relevancy and complexity of the thought unit.[41]

The question of reliability in the Taba study is an interesting one. Taba states the following as her procedure for estimating reliability:

> Instead of facing the problem of training an external jury of judges in the method of complex coding, a conference or a team method for coding was adopted. This consisted of the independent coding of a sample of tapescripts by two staff members who were responsible for developing the coding scheme. The differences were ironed out in conference until a consensus was reached or a correction was made in the coding system.[42]

Taba adds: "After the reliability of the codings was established, one of the staff members coded the remainder of the tapescripts, conferring with the other members whenever in doubt."[43]

Taba states that one of the two major problems in measuring reliability was agreement on division of the tapescripts into thought units. Now this is a serious problem because she earlier states that the coding of the level of thought depends upon the context. Therefore, it would seem that the division of the tapescript is crucial. Taba states that the check for reliability was done in one tapescript containing 336 thought units and that the two judges designating thought units on this one tapescript disagreed in less than 7 per cent of the cases. One judge coded 348 thought units; the other, 325 thought units.

As one studies Table XX (p. 141), one notices that the tapescript that has 388 thought units contains the fewest thought units of all twenty coded classes. Indeed, what is singularly striking is the range of thought units in these twenty reported classes, a range that begins with the low of 388 and ends with a high of 1,798. The total thought units for all twenty discussions was 18,821, with a mean of 941.05. Since 941.05 is plus 2.4 times as large as 388, one must ask whether the measure of reliability on the 388-unit tapescript can be extrapolated to the others under different conditions.

In discussing the codings of the thought units by her criteria, Taba reports that the two judges assigned the same ratings in 50 per cent of the thought units. She does not indicate whether or not some classifications were more stable than others; however, the fact that unreliability may have been concentrated in one area is suggested by this statement: "However, when the differentiation was reduced (i.e., when the 41 and 42 were combined) agreement between judges in-

[41] *Ibid.*, p. 199.
[42] *Ibid.*, p. 123.
[43] *Ibid.*, p. 123.

creased to 90 per cent. In the final analysis of the discussion data these codings were further combined to yield only three levels which would undoubtedly have even higher reliability."[44] No reason is offered for the further collapsing of the Taba category system, and no measure is offered as to the reliability of this collapsed system, reproduced in Table XV.

TABLE XV
Taba's Grouping of Thought Level Codings of the Three Cognitive Tasks into Three Levels of Cognitive Functioning

Cognitive Task	Level I	Level II	Level III
Grouping and labeling (Discussion 1)	11–22 Enumerating specific and general information	31–32 Grouping information	41+ Categorizing and labeling information
Interpreting information and making inferences (Discussions 2 and 3)	11–42 Enumerating, grouping, and categorizing	51–61 Giving reasons or making inferences	62+ Making inferences and stating cause and effect relationships. Stating principles
Predicting consequences and explaining new phenomena (Discussion 4)	121 and 221 Predicting and explaining without rationale	101–102 201–202 111 and 211 122 and 222 Giving information that establishes parameters. Giving conditions. Predicting or explaining with reasons, etc.	112 and 212 123 and 223 Stating conditions and establishing logical connections. Predicting accompanied by stated or implied principle.

From Hilda Taba and others, "Thinking in Elementary School Children," p. 153.

Taba developed a graphic representation of her coding that charts the transactions between the teacher and the children, the changes in the level of thought during a discussion, and the effect of these strategies on the level and direction of thought. This graphic presentation is shown in Figure 7. Her explanation of this flowchart is:

> In this flowchart, the thought units were represented by equal intervals on the horizontal axis, and their level on the vertical axis. Thus, the systematic progression of the thought units and the relative

[44] *Ibid.*, p. 123.

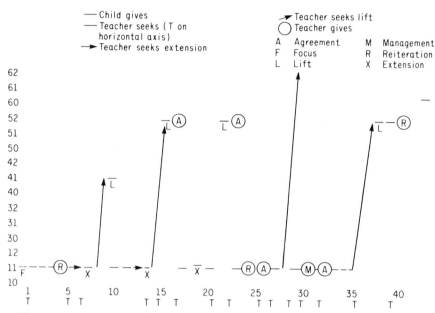

Figure 7. Taba's flowchart of classroom interaction (modified). (From Hilda Taba and others, "Thinking in Elementary School Children," p. 125.)

levels of thought can be presented diagrammatically. The thought units of the teacher are indicated by "T" along the horizontal axis. The horizontal arrows, such as appear for thought units 7 and 13, represent the teacher's request for an extension of thought expressed just prior to these units. The vertical arrows shown for thought units 9, 15, 28, and 36 depict the teacher's attempts to lift the thought to a higher level. Thought unit 10 (L) indicated that the child complied with the teacher's request for a lift in level and produced a thought unit at the 41 level. The other letters represent other function codings such as reiteration, approval, agreements, etc.[45]

In analyzing her data, Taba presents, in addition to the thought units per class, the percentages of thought units for the children and teachers. She also presents percentages for teachers in the use of the groups of functions enumerated earlier. Further analyses were performed on the data in order to "... determine the relationship between the level of difficulty and the nature of the cognitive task, a chi square test was performed using the frequencies of responses at the three cognitive levels for the four discussions for all grades combined."[46] Additionally, chi square tests were conducted to determine if there was a relationship between level of thought and the grade level.

Data on participation of children were secured. Children were

[45] *Ibid.*, p. 124.
[46] *Ibid.*, p. 155.

characterized as having either "low" or "high" participation scores. These classifications were determined by finding out the median percentage of participation for each class and classifying all children whose participation percentage was below the class mean as low participators and all those whose percentage of participation was above the mean as high participators. Participation was undefined in the study.

After determining the amount of a child's participation, the level of his participation was computed. Percentages of each child's thought units were calculated for each of the three cognitive tasks: "The highest level at which a child's percentages exceed the class percentage was designated his typical level."[47] Thus, each child was classified on two dimensions: his amount of participation and typical thought level. Six categories disclose the possibilities of the scheme:

A	High thought level	High participation
B	High thought level	Low participation
C	Middle thought level	High participation
D	Middle thought level	Low participation
E	Low thought level	High participation
F	Low thought level	Low participation[48]

Chi square tests were performed and gamma correlation coefficients were computed for each of the four discussions.[49]

One final analysis was made to determine if there was a relationship between performance in classroom discussion and scores on the social studies inference test: "The children in each of the classes were divided into high and low scorers on each of the four subtests of the Social Studies Inference Test and chi square tests were performed between the frequencies of high scorers of the test as related to performance in discussion."[50]

It is quite apparent from even a cursory perusal of the Flanders and Taba category systems that they are both so singular that they are unlike any of the others being examined here. Both the Bellack and Smith category systems attempt to deal with language and logic in the classroom. Although there is a similarity of orientation, since their unit of analysis is different, their systems as developed bear little resemblance to one another. On the other hand, Bellack and Hughes both use a functional unit of analysis, but their different orientation results in entirely different systems of analysis. More will be said of the Bellack and Hughes and Bellack and Smith systems in answering question six, which is being dealt with in Chapter XII.

[47]*Ibid.*, p. 158.
[48]*Ibid.*, p. 161.
[49]*Ibid.*, p. 162.
[50]*Ibid.*, p. 163.

XII

Categorizing the Studies in Terms of Specific Characteristics

A discussion of specific characteristics of the studies will include review, assessment, and explication of some of the statements made earlier about relationships existing between and among these studies. This review may serve the purposes of clarification as well as preparation for discussion of the crucial final issues.

Many different relationships exist between and among these studies, and one could find relationships existing between any one of them and any or all of the other four. However, only a discussion of the relationships existing between the following five combinations of studies will be detailed: (1) Flanders and Hughes, (2) Flanders and Taba, (3) Bellack and Hughes, (4) Bellack and Smith, and (5) Smith and Taba.

The great similarities between the Flanders and Hughes studies are in their shared theoretical roots and in the similarity of their assumptions and interest. Both are interested in the interaction of teacher with student; both hypothesize the teacher as the central power figure in the classroom; both hold the teacher to be responsible for the patterns of influence that develop throughout the class, and both are non-content-oriented.

The similarity between the Flanders and Taba studies is less obvious, but both studies suggest that certain kinds of teacher behavior will bring about certain kinds of results in student performance. Flanders, in a hypothesis testing study, assesses the relationship between teacher influence and student learning. Taba, in a more loosely designed study, suggests that the levels of student thought can be raised as a result of coupling certain kinds of curriculum experiences with certain kinds of teaching techniques. Both studies use an original measuring instrument as a tool central to the findings of their study; Flanders uses this instrument in his first year study. The development and use of these measuring instruments will be explored here.

At the core of the Flanders conceptual scheme lies the concept of indirect and direct teacher influence. It is Flanders' notion that indirect teacher influence encourages student independence and greater student learning, just as direct teacher influence produces greater student dependence and less student learning. However, Flanders believes that certain students have greater dependency needs than others. To control this variable of what was to be termed "dependency-proneness," a test was developed. The method for item development and initial validation is described by Flanders:

> The previous research on dependence indicated that a scale of dependence proneness should include items that describe students who are complying to adults and conforming to group pressures. Our staff wrote, borrowed, and modified 150 items to form an initial battery. These items were set either in the social context of peer relationships—that is, contacts with fellow students and student leaders, or adult-child relationships—that is, with parents, teachers and other adult authority figures. The themes of the items were either seeking help, succor, affection and affiliation, or conformity, compliance, and seeking approval.
>
> The 150-item battery was administered to 1,245 students in classes selected at random from the total population of eighth grade homerooms in the combined school systems of Minneapolis and St. Paul. These tests were scored by an arbitrary key. The response to each item was restricted to "agree" or "disagree."
>
> Four separate item analyses were performed to isolate 45 items that appear in the final scale. One item analysis made use of the different reactions of students nominated by teachers as dependent and independent. A second analysis made use of students who shifted counter to the intended influence. The fourth analysis made use of the top and bottom groups formed by the total score of all 150 items.[1]

Thirty-three teachers whose classes were taking the 150-item test were given a form containing two paragraphs. One paragraph contained a small case study depicting the actions of the type of child Flanders would classify as dependent, the other, those of the type of child classified as independent. Flanders describes the next steps: "The teachers were asked to list eight names in connection with each paragraph. Four names were listed in rank order as being most like the paragraph and four names were listed in rank order as being least like the paragraph."[2]

---

[1] Ned A. Flanders, "Teacher Influence, Pupil Attitudes, and Achievement: Studies in Interaction Analysis," U.S. Office of Education Cooperative Research Project No. 397 (Minneapolis: University of Minnesota, 1960), Appendix E, p. 2.

[2] *Ibid.*, Appendix E, p. 3.

A second form was then sent to the teachers explaining in greater detail the purposes behind the securing of the data, and the teachers were then asked again to nominate names in terms of dependence and independence. Greater weight was given to those names that appear on the first and second teachers' list in conducting the item analysis.

A second procedure was to develop an influence technique system that would determine those students whose opinions could most easily be swayed. To accomplish this end a tape-recorded procedure was devised:

> Ten opinion items, read by a narrator, were reproduced from a tape recording to which students responded by marking their answer sheets on a nine-point scale from strongly agree to strongly disagree. Items were developed and modified in pilot runs so that the initial reactions of eighth grade students would be relatively homogeneous and predictable .... The answer sheets were collected, and the students learned that just before marking the same items again they would hear the opinion of a famous expert recorded for radio, TV or by special request. Before each student marked his second answers, a short but strong argument was heard.[3]

Student papers were collected, and then the opposite side of the argument was heard, and again the students were asked to mark their opinions. Total shift scores were used to calculate changes in the intended direction and changes away from the intended direction. There were 423 students involved in the persuasion experiments. Another analysis was based on only those 100 students or the 8.05 per cent at the top and bottom of the group as determined by the total 150 original item score. The final 45-item test was prepared when "... the results of at least two of the preceding item analysis procedures showed promise."[4]

Contrast the development of the Flanders test with that of the Taba Social Studies Inference Test. Taba states the test items were written around a sample of generalizations for each grade level from two through six. Four scores were to be provided: inference (I), discrimination (D), caution (C), and overgeneralization (OG). These items were reviewed by subject matter supervisors and the faculty of San Francisco State College who train teachers in the social studies.

Taba reports the following pre-testing procedures:

> (a) Group testing—the situation was administered to a group of older subjects who had completed the grades to which the generalizations apply. This procedure was helpful in weeding out ambiguous, irrelevant, and overly difficult items.

[3] *Ibid.*, Appendix E, p. 4.
[4] *Ibid.*

(b) Individual testing—at various states in the initial development of the test, individual children were asked to respond to the situations. They read the situations out loud and judged each inference as Probably True, Probably False, or Can't Tell. They were then asked to give a rationale for the answer they selected. This entire procedure was tape recorded and provided a check on the ease of readability, vocabulary level, and whether children provide appropriate generalizations for explaining their choices.[5]

During one of the training courses, teachers were asked to make judgments on their children's ability to make inferences. These teacher judgments were correlated with the results of the post-test on the Social Studies Inference Test. The results are shown in Table XVI.

TABLE XVI

Taba's Gamma Correlation Coefficients between Teacher's
Judgment of Children's Ability to Make Inferences
and Social Studies Inference Post-Test Scores

Teacher	Grade							
	N	3rd	N	4th	N	5th	N	6th
A	22	.33	16	.63^a	27	.73^a	21	.00
B	23	.51	23	.29	26	.22	25	.29
C	32	.26	20	.27	21	.64^a	27	.28
D	31	-.32			20	.60^a	28	.38
E	20	-.15			25	.15		

From Hilda Taba and others, "Thinking in Elementary School Children," p. 89.
^{a}P .05.

Taba reports the following relationship between her test and other measures of ability: "Perhaps the most startling finding of the study was the generally low relationship between the level of thinking and any of the traditionally influential variables: intelligence, achievement in social studies, reading comprehension, and social status."[6]

Flanders reports both confirmation of his test findings and also areas of difficulties. Britton, using a similar technique of teacher nomination of dependent and independent students, failed to produce evidence of predicted differences in student behavior. Additionally, a positive correlation ranging from +0.19 to +0.44 was shown to exist between the measure of dependency and IQ and was reported as a possible flaw in the test. Thus, even a test as carefully prepared

[5] Hilda Taba and others, "Thinking in Elementary School Children," U.S. Department of Health, Education, and Welfare, Cooperative Research Program, Project No. 1574 (San Francisco: San Francisco State College, 1964), p. 85.
[6] *Ibid.*, p. 175.

as the Flanders test, in which only one of two possible identifications was to be made, reports difficulty in validation and use.

One must note that, although Taba reports startlingly low correlations between the Social Studies Inference Test and intelligence, achievement in social studies, reading comprehension, social status, and teacher judgments, she does not hesitate to use the findings. Remembering that the Flanders test seeks to make one judgment and reports difficulty accomplishing that end, one must wonder at Taba's use of her test to make four judgments and to assess growth with evidence neither of correlation with IQ, achievement, or teacher judgment nor item validation nor evidence as to what growth would be expected in a year's time. Although the Flanders and Taba studies illustrate the development of a unique measuring instrument, they illustrate two entirely different approaches to the problem.

Bellack and Hughes have one specific characteristic in common— their use of a functional unit of analysis. In making the decision as to how classroom discourse would be analyzed, Bellack decided on a unit of analysis that served a pedagogical function. He described four pedagogical functions: soliciting, structuring, responding, and reacting, and analyzed his data in terms of these functions. Although Hughes shares with Bellack the functional unit of analysis, she defined function differently. Hughes sees function as an act of the teachers, and, in coding a particular function, the question is raised as to what function this act served for a child, group, or class.

The Bellack and Smith studies share a concentration on language and logic. Although Smith's study is called "The Logic of Teaching," Bellack's study may more nearly disclose the logic of teaching than does Smith's. In attempting to superimpose the canons of formal logic on the teaching language, Smith obscures what might be a logic that is unique to the teaching enterprise. While Bellack too uses the categories of logic, most notably in his more detailed analysis of the soliciting act, his study more nearly reveals the actual logic of the teaching process with its detailing of the pedagogical moves than does Smith's. Another characteristic that the Bellack and Smith studies share is a characteristic of their coding system. As Smith speaks of coding an entry in terms of an "ideal" response, Bellack discusses the expectation of response and respondents.

Taba and Smith use a similar unit of analysis. Although Taba, in her list of three requirements for her multidimensional analysis system, lists the need to code teaching behavior in terms of the pedagogical function it serves in developing student cognitive behavior, reminiscent of Bellack's unit of analysis, Taba identifies her basic unit as the "thought unit," which is defined as: ". . . a remark or series of remarks which expresses a more or less complete idea, serves a specified function and can be classified by a level of thought."[7] Smith's definition of a venture, while not completely congruent with Taba's "thought unit," is of the same character: "A venture is a segment of discourse consisting of a set of utterances dealing with a single topic and having a single overarching content objective."[8]

Taba's basic thesis is that the level of thinking of students can be raised when appropriate curriculum experiences are coupled with proper teaching techniques. Smith, too, is interested in improved student thinking and suggests that a more proper use of the categories of logic in the classroom would improve the student level of performance.

[7] *Ibid.*, p. 115.

[8] B. Othanel Smith and Milton O. Meux, "A Tentative Report on Strategies of Teaching," U.S. Office of Education, Department of Health, Education, and Welfare, Project No. 1640 (Urbana: Bureau of Educational Research, College of Education, University of Illinois, 1964), p. 5.

XIII

The Effectiveness of
the Studies

Before attempting to deal with the effectiveness of the studies, a comment must be made on the evaluative possibilities of these studies. Except for Flanders, who presents hypotheses to be tested in both his first and second year studies, the studies do not easily lend themselves to evaluation in terms of the problems or questions with which they deal. All the other four studies enter disclaimers which indicate that the study is either exploratory or in some sense tentative. Therefore, it is not to be expected that these studies will fulfill the standards of reliability and validity to which studies in other areas are held. However, whether tentative or exploratory in nature, these studies have been published, and it is not expected that they can or should pass without some kind of evaluative comment.

The first part of the Bellack study focused on the development of a unit of analysis of instruction, on the development of measures of learning and attitude change, and on the development of a content analysis system.

Bellack's category system was developed to function with a high degree of reliability. However, his study showed no particular relationships between classroom variables and the outcome variables as were developed in the tests of knowledge and attitude change. Since the research staff prepared the tests of knowledge, and Bellack reports great content variation among the presentations of the various teachers, it may be that for some classes the test was a fairer judge of the material taught than for other classes. It might have been valuable to have had the individual teachers prepare and give their own tests. Then one might have been in a position to compare the content covered by the teacher-made tests with those of the research staff, as well as to compare the difference in student scores between the teacher-made tests and the research staff's test. The design of the test itself, if novel in design for some students and common in design for others, might have affected the results.

A seven point attitude scale was developed to measure the students' attitudes toward the studying of economics. Originally the statements ran from very negative to very positive. Since students did not select the entirely negative statements these were removed as they served no discriminating function. The attitude scale was revised to run from relatively neutral comments to very positive ones. Since there is normally a trend to the center in attitude test taking, perhaps the removal of the most negative items forced the students further up the attitude scale than they would have gone had the negative statements remained. It may be, as Bellack suggests, that outcome variables in classroom study will have to be carefully and systematically explicated in the future as the process variables.

Below are some of the findings that were derived from the use of the category system developed in the first part of the Bellack study:

1. The teacher-pupil ratio of activity in terms of lines spoken is approximately 3 to 1; in terms of moves this ratio is about 3 to 2. Therefore, regardless of the unit considered, teachers are considerably more active than pupils in amount of verbal activity.

2. The pedagogical roles of the classroom are clearly delineated for teachers and pupils. Teachers are responsible for structuring the lesson, soliciting responses from pupils, reacting to pupils' responses, and, to some extent, summarizing aspects of the discourse. The pupil's primary task is to respond to the teacher's solicitations. Occasionally, pupils react to preceding statements, but these reactions are rarely evaluative. Pupils do not overtly react evaluatively to the teacher's statements, and they evaluate other pupils' responses only when the teacher asks them to do so. There are deviations from this pattern, but they are infrequent. By and large, pupils do not solicit responses from the teacher about substantive meanings. When pupils do solicit, the solicitations usually concern instructional matters, such as asking for clarification of an assignment or explanation of a classroom procedure. Pupils do not spontaneously structure the discourse; their structuring moves are almost always response to specific assignments made by the teacher, and usually involve debates or reports.[1]

In the second part of the Bellack study, the system of analysis was both refined and combined. This development of the category system was detailed in question 5 and will be commented upon again in question 8. Here it might be of value to reproduce what Bellack describes as the five general rules of play for teacher and pupil in the classroom game.

1. The basic verbal maneuvers that the teacher and the pupil make in playing the game are pedagogical moves: structuring and soliciting, which are initiatory moves; and responding and reacting, which are reflexive moves. Each of the four types of moves plays a distinctive role in the discourse. Soliciting, responding, and reacting each accounts for

[1] Arno A. Bellack and Joel R. Davitz, *The Language of the Classroom*, U.S. Department of Health, Education and Welfare, Cooperative Research Program, Project No. 1497, (New York, Institute of Psychological Research, Teachers College, Columbia University, 1963), p. 84.

slightly less than one-third of the moves in a given classroom, and structuring accounts for the remaining small fraction of moves. In terms of amount of speech (i.e., lines of transcript), reacting accounts for three-eighths of the lines spoken, and the remaining five-eighths is just about equally distributed among the remaining three moves.

2. The teacher is the most active player in the game. He makes the most moves; he speaks most frequently; and his speeches usually are the longest. He is permitted some flexibility in the exact amount by which his activity exceeds the total activity of all pupil players, but in general the ratio of his speech to the speech of all other players is approximately 3 to 1 in terms of lines spoken, and 3 to 2 in terms of the number of moves made. Moreover, these ratios remain constant over several class sessions, unless the teacher directs another player to assume his role temporarily.

3. If the game is played within the field of economics, the major part of the game is played with substantive meanings specified by the teacher's structuring of the game. From time to time, however, players are permitted to depart from this central focus, sometimes to topics tangential to the substantive material of the game and occasionally to a topic that is irrelevant to the subject matter under study. The teacher usually initiates these off-target discussions, sometimes as a means of introducing a substantive point. Occasionally, a pupil player introduces an irrelevancy, but he does not do so often in a single class session; the exact frequency depends upon the reactions of the teacher. In general, however, the discussion takes place within the substantive framework of the teacher's structuring.

4. Players generally use the empirical mode of thought (fact stating and explaining) in dealing with the substantive material under discussion. The analytic mode (defining terms and interpreting statements) is used much less frequently. The frequency of evaluative statements (opining and justifying) is also relatively low in comparison to empirical statements; that is, expressions of personal opinion about economic policies or attempts to justify opinions appear rather infrequently. However, players are free to report opinions of others, such as public officials, or to report the arguments used by others to justify their opinions. This does not mean that players are completely prohibited from expressing their own opinions and justifications, but that the general rules under which the game is played encourage the use of the empirical mode of thought.

5. In gauging wins and losses, players should keep in mind that this is not a game in which one player, such as the teacher, wins, while another player, such as one of the pupils, loses. Rather, there are relative degrees of winning and losing, and the teacher's winnings are a function of the pupil's performances. This is a peculiar, but important, characteristic of this game. While the teacher undeniably has the greater power and freedom in the course of play, he is ultimately dependent on his pupils for the degree of success he achieves in playing the game.[2]

Listed below are the three major hypotheses of the first year

---

[2] Arno A. Bellack, *The Language of the Classroom*, U.S. Department of Health, Education and Welfare, Cooperative Research Program, Project No. 2023, (New York, Institute of Psychological Research, Teachers College, Columbia University, 1965), p. 238.

Flanders study:

(1.0) Direct teacher influence restricts learning when a student's perception of the goal is confused and ambiguous.

(2.0) Direct teacher influence increases learning when a student's perception of the goal is clear and acceptable.

(3.0) Indirect teacher influence increases learning when a student's perception of the goal is confused and ambiguous.

It was proposed that the analysis of any data relevant to the support or rejection of these hypotheses be analyzed separately for gifted, average, and below average students. A Ph.D. thesis study, carried out by Dr. Edmund Amidon permits us to report the analysis of data separately for students scoring high and low on the dependence proneness test for the first year laboratory experiments.[3]

The following statements are made concerning the results of this experiment:

We, conclude that teacher influence cannot account for any differences that may occur between the goal clear and goal ambiguous treatments in either subject matter area.[4]

For over four years we have found it difficult to obtain any measure of goal perception from students under field conditions.[5]

Many of the expected significant outcomes of the first year failed to appear, but for each hypothesis relevant data from the second year supplied the necessary support. In no instances are there significant outcomes that reject any of the theoretical propositions of the study.[6]

It might be appropriate to discuss, at this juncture, one aspect of the first year laboratory experiments in which one teacher was trained to use both a direct and indirect pattern of influence. Teacher direct influence was used in experimental groups I and III, and teacher indirect influence was used in groups II and IV. If one peruses the interaction tallies, shown in Table XVII, one notes the sizable differences in the interaction patterns of these two groups in such areas as student talk and direct and indirect teacher talk. It is also obvious that different patterns of teaching were produced.

What is of interest is the comparison of the behavior of the trained teachers of the first year laboratory study with the "natural" direct and indirect teachers who show no such similar patterns of interaction. Indeed, in Table XVIII which shows some of the second year field study results the students spoke more in classes where there were direct teachers than in classes where there are indirect teachers.

[3] Ned A. Flanders, *Teacher Influence, Pupil Attitudes, and Achievement: Studies in Interaction Analysis, U.S.* Office of Education Cooperative Research Project No. 397, (Minneapolis, University of Minnesota, 1960), p. 19.

[4] *Ibid.*, p. 29.

[5] *Ibid.*, p. 33.

[6] *Ibid.*, p. 80.

TABLE XVII

Flanders First Year Study Per Cent of Tallies in Interaction
Categories During Period IV

Categories	Geometry Experimental Treatment				Social Studies Experimental Treatment			
	I	III	II	IV	I	III	II	IV
Indirect 1, 2	1.61	1.35	14.90	17.04	. . .	0.14	8.45	7.98
Teacher 3	0.92	2.48	16.10	15.78	2.74	1.97	14.24	16.34
Talk 4	1.73	2.58	30.04	28.07	3.16	3.52	20.90	22.60
Direct 5	61.40	63.10	15.97	13.52	70.80	71.40	27.25	23.58
Teacher 6	10.36	8.67	0.27	0.28	4.12	5.50	2.66	1.60
Talk 7	15.54	13.03	0.94	1.27	6.17	6.48	0.85	0.61
Student Talk 8, 9	5.07	5.29	17.17	16.47	10.00	5.78	22.95	25.30
Silence 10	3.45	3.49	4.69	7.75	0.41	5.08	2.65	2.22
TOTAL TALLIES	869	889	746	711	730	709	828	815

Ned A. Flanders, "Teacher Influence, Pupil Attitudes, and Achievement," p. 28.

TABLE XVIII

Flanders' Second Year Study Per Cent Teacher Talk,
Student Talk, and Silence for Direct
and Indirect Teachers

Condition	Mathematics		Social Studies	
	Indirect	Direct	Indirect	Direct
Teacher talk	74.6	67.4	63.8	55.9
Student talk	16.8	19.8	27.0	30.2
Silence	9.6	12.8	9.2	13.9

From Ned A. Flanders, "Teacher Influence, Pupil Attitudes, and
Achievement," p. 57.

These findings raise the question of the validity of training teachers
to behave in a fashion that is foreign to their own "natural" style and
seemingly equally foreign to the "natural" classroom style.

In Flanders' second year study, he reports greater achievement
for students in both the social studies and mathematics classes based
on the teacher i/d ratio. An interesting aspect of the Flanders study
is the grouping of his classes on the basis of the "natural" direct or
indirect influence as progress toward learning goals occurs.[7]

Caution in evaluating the findings concerning teacher flexibility
is to be urged since no reliability is reported for the unit of analysis
upon which the flexibility findings are based.

Although at the inception of the Hughes study the question was
raised as to what were the differences in pattern of behavior between

[7] *Ibid.*, p. 104.

the judged-good teachers and the representative teachers, no differences were found. Following is a summary of the analysis of the Hughes data:

> There are no differences between the Judged-good teachers and the Representative teachers from one school.
> When teachers are grouped according to deviations from the mean into three groups of nine, statistical differences are located. (Two members of the "good" group were from Representative teachers.) The four categories that differentiate the "good" from the "poor" groups are Controlling, Functions That Develop Content, Personal Response, and Negative Affectivity. The only difference between the "good" and the "middle" groups is in Personal Response.
> There are differences between eleven primary teachers (first and second) and eleven intermediate grade teachers (fifth and sixth).
> The primary teachers are more controlling, more negative, and perform a larger number of teaching acts in the ninety-minute period of observation.
> There are differences between situations according to content.
> The teachers use Controlling Functions significantly less in the Activity period than with the other content situations; also, they use more Functions of Personal Response.
> Less use of Functions of Negative Affectivity is found in the Social Studies period.
> When the analysis of variance is used with order of observation, which randomizes content, the thirty-five teachers differ significantly from one another in the categories of Imposition, Functions That Develop Content, Positive Affectivity, and Negative Affectivity.
> Teachers differ from one another on the Dominative Behavior Index at the .05 level of significance and differ from one another on the Integrative Behavior Index at the .001 level of significance.
> A relatively few teachers at either end of the distribution on any one of the indices used contributed to the significant differences noted.
> Intercorrelations of categories according to situations and with total across situations are suggestive:
>
> Personal Response is correlated negatively with Controlling;
>
> Personal Response is correlated negatively with Negative Affectivity;
>
> Personal Response is correlated positively with Facilitating;
>
> Content Development is correlated positively with Positive Affectivity.[8]

One of the questions posed at the outset of the study was, "What is Good Teaching?" Hughes answered that by stating her views on the subject and constructing a model in terms of percentages of teacher functions that satisfied her own criteria. Thus, when Hughes speaks of "good," "middle," and "poor" teachers, these judgments derive from her own model. The only question posed at the study's

[8] Marie M. Hughes and Associates, "The Assessment of the Quality of Teaching: A Research Report," U.S. Office of Education Cooperative Research Project No. 353 (Salt Lake City: University of Utah, 1959), p. 283.

inception that was successfully answered concerned the differences in teacher behavior according to the content situation. Hughes was able to show that such a difference in behavior did exist.

Both of Smith's studies deal with the development of a system of analysis for classroom discourse. Since this is his major focus, a more detailed discussion of Smith's category system will be found in the answer to Chapter XIV. Only one point will be made here, and that has to do with the effect of unreliability of categories and their effect on analysis. Only in his first study does Smith attempt to analyze his tapescripts in terms of his proposed categories of logical episodes. The following paragraph illustrates the kinds of conclusions Smith offers in this first study:

> Within the science area, physiology is more concerned with Defining (1.12) and Designating (3.13) than the other subjects; physics is concerned more with the use of symbols (1.14) and Conditional Inferring; biology and chemistry deal more with Evaluating (correctness of evidence, correct answers to problems, etc.) than with either physics or physiology.[9]

When one checks Smith's reliability tables, one learns that while the category of Defining 1.12 has a reliability coefficient of .88, Designating has a reliability coefficient of .48, and the category that is supposed to describe the central concern of physics has a reliability coefficient of .00.

Since the chief focus of the Taba study was the effect of training on the development of thought, it is unfortunate that so little evidence is offered to make a proper judgment on the results of her study. The problems surrounding the assumptions Taba makes on the hierarchical nature of thinking have already been explicated, as have the problems concerning the identification of her unit of analysis and those concerning her test development. Only two additional points need to be raised. On the basis of four observations during an entire year of schooling, one can have little information on what kinds of teaching techniques were used and what kinds of curriculum were followed during the other times of the year. The design of the Taba study precluded a successful answer to the question of the effect of training on thought. No valid and reliable measures of thought were indicated at the beginning of the study; therefore, even had growth in thinking taken place in excess of what is normally expected within the course of a year, there would have been no way to measure this growth.

Some of the major results that Taba reports are shown in Tables XIX and XX.

[9] B. Othanel Smith and Milton O. Meux, "A Study of the Logic of Teaching" (Urbana: Bureau of Educational Research, College of Education, University of Illinois, 1963), p. 53.

TABLE XIX

Taba's Observed (O) and Expected (E) Frequencies of Children Falling
into the Six Categories of Performance for Each of
the Four Discussions

Thought Level	Participation	Category	Discussion 1		Discussion 2		Discussion 3		Discussion 4	
			O	E	O	E	O	E	O	E
III	High	A	68	54	47	38	62	47	39	30
	Low	B	41	55	40	49	30	44	15	24
II	High	C	21	15	59	58	66	62	69	61
	Low	D	9	15	74	75	54	58	42	50
I	High	E	89	109	54	64	63	82	60	77
	Low	F	129	109	93	83	96	77	81	64

From Hilda Taba and others, "Thinking in Elementary School Children," p. 162.

TABLE XX

Taba's Percentages of Thought Units That Are Classified as Child Gives,
Teacher Seeks, Teacher Gives, and Child Seeks

	Total Units	Percentages					
		CG	TS	TG	CS	Child	Teacher
1st Discussion							
2nd Grades	580	56	25	19	0	56	44
3rd Grades	1,338	54	24	22	0	54	46
4th Grades	480	55	21	23	1	56	44
5th Grades	388	65	18	16	1	66	34
6th Grades	1,400	47	21	30	2	49	51
Total	4,186	53	22	24	1	54	46
2nd Discussion							
2nd Grades	687	55	27	17	1	56	44
3rd Grades	1,322	52	28	17	3	55	45
4th Grades	539	67	23	9	1	68	32
5th Grades	987	66	26	7	2	68	33
6th Grades	964	57	25	18	0	57	42
Total	4,499	58	26	14	2	60	40
3rd Discussion							
2nd Grades	805	55	29	16	1	56	44
3rd Grades	981	59	28	14	0	59	42
4th Grades	636	60	28	12	0	60	40
5th Grades	1,125	64	27	9	0	64	36
6th Grades	1,798	50	30	19	1	51	49
Total	5,345	56	28	15	1	57	43
4th Discussion							
2nd Grades	864	52	25	22	0	52	47
3rd Grades	1,185	57	28	15	0	61	43
4th Grades	459	61	24	15	0	61	39
5th Grades	1,405	60	29	9	2	62	38
6th Grades	878	67	18	12	2	69	30
Total	4,791	59	26	14	1	60	40
Totals	18,821	57	26	16	1	58	42

From Hilda Taba and others, "Thinking in Elementary School Children," p. 139.

XIV

Possibilities of a General System for Observation and Analysis

Category systems are built upon some system of content analysis. Content analysis makes possible the handling of data normally unsusceptible to analysis, and thus quantification is possible. In the content analysis process total statements and responses are divided into elements that are meaningful within a particular system. Statements and situations occasionally have to be coded that do not fit within an a priori established system. Flanders describes such an incident:

> ... After five years of experience, for example, the writer was stumped by a teacher who spontaneously started to role play a student in the library using the general catalog. The teacher wanted to summarize a lesson in how to use the library for reference purposes. Her actions were both humorous and informative. She asked a student what topic he expected to look up during the class's impending first library visit, and pretended to thumb through a series of cards, reading imaginary topics, some of which were very funny. "Oh dear!" she said, "There is nothing on crocodiles. What shall I do now?" "Try reptiles," said a brighter student. As the little dramatization developed, the class learned how to make cross references. After discussing the incident with the observer team, we decided that the teacher's primary intent was to develop a problem in terms of the students' experience, that the teacher was working with an anticipated student problem, and that the humor encouraged both present and future participation. The decision was to classify most of the role playing in category three with the humorous parts in category two.[1]

Thus a choice is made; either the categories are constantly widened to include more and more different kinds of information, and thus become increasingly more abstract, or categories go through a process of division and redefinition in order to capture what are con-

[1] Ned A. Flanders, "Teacher Influence, Pupil Attitudes, and Achievement: Studies in Interaction Analysis," U.S. Office of Education Cooperative Research Project No. 397 (Minneapolis: University of Minnesota, 1960), Appendix F, p. 9.

sidered by the category designer to be the "meaningful differences." The latter solution leads to a multiplication of categories that can often render the system so unwieldy as to become unreliable and of little use.

The Flanders system divides classroom interaction into ten categories. One of these categories is noise or confusion, two refer to pupil participation, and seven of them represent teacher talk. In Flanders' study, he presents his total interaction patterns for indirect and direct teachers of mathematics and for indirect and direct teachers of social studies. Four interaction matrices can be found from pages 52 to 55[2]. If one notes just the 5 × 5 cell in each of the four matrices, one observes that of the 1,000 tallies, indirect mathematics teachers have 383.9 tallies in the 5 × 5 cell; the direct mathematics teachers have 312.9 tallies out of a possible 1,000 in the 5 × 5 cell. Observing the interaction matrices of the social studies teachers, one finds that the indirect social studies teachers have 310.6 tallies in the 5 × 5 cell out of a possible 1,000 tallies and the direct social studies teachers have 170.4 tallies in the 5 × 5 cell out of a possible 1,000 tallies. Thus, in two totaled interaction matrices the tallies in one of the possible hundred cells accounts for close to one third of the totaled possible tallies, and in one case the totaled tallies exceed one third of all the possible totaled tallies.

It may be of interest here to define again Flanders' category 5, since the 5 × 5 cell represents 5 followed by 5: "(5) Lecturing: gives facts or opinions about content or procedures; expressing his own ideas, asking rhetorical questions."[3]

Of course, since Flanders is interested in charting "classroom climate," it may be that these categories, although broad, are sufficient to the task. However, when a discussion of a general classificatory system is raised, one must observe that the grouping of so many aspects of classroom discourse into one category—5, in this case— may render the category so abstract as to limit seriously the amount of information it is capable of delivering.

As Flanders' system may be too abstract, Smith's system may be too particularized. In coding his first unit of analysis, the *episode*, Smith has 94 discrete classifications. For purposes of testing the reliability of his categories, Smith collapses many of the categories. Although enumerating 31 separate types of *Describing*, he presents one reliability rating for the entire class. One reliability score is presented for *Stating*, for which five separate designations were made.

[2] Page numbers given are those in the Flanders study.
[3] Ned A. Flanders, "Teacher Influence, Pupil Attitudes, and Achievement," Appendix F, p. 5.

Other categories collapsed into one for purposes of reporting reliability were: *Substituting, Evaluating, Opining, Classifying, Comparing* and *Contrasting*, and *Conditional Inferring*. After collapsing the categories, Smith's reliability range is still broad. A .33 reliability is reported for *Reporting* and the highest reliability reported is for *Substituting*, .88. In Smith's other categories—*Defining, Designating*, and *Explaining*—a complete set of reliability scores is presented for the first two and a partial set of reliability scores is presented for the last, *Explaining*. In these categories, Smith's reliability range is from .00 in Defining (4) to 1.00 in *Designating* (5).

In Smith's second study he identifies a unit called the venture. Smith identifies nine ventures. In his reported reliability of venture identification, his reliability range is from .00 in the identification of *Causal* ventures to 1.00 in the identification of *Systems* ventures. Smith takes one venture, the *Conceptual* venture, on which he has a reported reliability of .75, and identifies eighteen kinds of moves that characterize a *Conceptual* venture. No reliability is reported for the identification of these eighteen moves.

If Flanders' system is too abstract to deliver all the information that might make classroom analysis meaningful, Smith's system may be seen as too detailed and unwieldy to be used with reliability. The kind of unit of analysis used by Smith, which depends upon judgments as to content objectives, may be at the root of Smith's reliability problems. The knotty judgment aspect of the Smith category system is true also of the Taba system, and may account for the fact that Taba does not even report specific reliability measures on individual aspects of her code and, in the final use of her code, collapses many of her original distinctions.

The Taba code, with its questionable reliability even in the basic unit discrimination and with its reflection of Taba's unsupported scheme of hierarchical pattern of thought, does not seem to be usable for research purposes that are outside of the total Taba framework.

The Hughes code seems a workable one, for which rather respectable reliability is reported, ranging from a low of 62.6 per cent in the *Imposition* category to a high of 87.8 per cent in the *Controlling* category.

In reporting reliability in the category system used in Bellack's first part of his study, his lowest reported reliability is .84 in per cent of agreement of lines in instructional-logical meaning; his highest reliability is .96 in per cent of agreement of lines in substantive meanings.

Bellack and Hughes both use a functional unit of analysis that may be inherently more reliable than the kind of unit of analysis used by both Smith and Taba, which requires judgments on the purpose a unit serves in a particular context.

The Hughes code, like the Flanders code, concentrates on the teacher and on climate. Neither code was established to reveal content structure, language, or logical patterns. Both Hughes and Flanders have systems that incorporate a point of view, and their codes may not be useful to the researcher who does not share their theoretical framework.

The Bellack system, which too has assumptions, is nonetheless the least theoretically encumbered system, with the possible exception of Smith's. Bellack's system is highly reliable; capable of rendering detailed information as to language, logic, and content; and capable of indicating sequences and patterns of behavior through the time dimension. Of course, the content in the Bellack study was controlled, and it may be that noncontrolled content would not as readily yield itself to classification with the Bellack system. The more detailed analysis of the pedagogical move presented in Bellack's second part of his study, especially in his analysis of the soliciting and structuring moves, appears to be too discrete and particularized. Thus the structuring move, one of the four pedagogical moves, is divided into three major categories: (1) the persons involved in the soliciting act; (2) the indicative meaning of the soliciting move: the activities the solicitor directs an agent to perform; and (3) the stylistic meaning of the soliciting move: the manner of presenting the move. Under each of the three major categories there is a further subdivision which, in the case of the indicative meaning of the soliciting move, includes five divisions. These second subdivisions are again subdivided at least once, twice, and in some cases three more times. This great detailing, however, does not appear to have cost Bellack any loss of reliability.

Bellack has systematically worked in two directions in his coding scheme: first, toward greater detailed analysis, and second, toward larger and larger combinations of units of analysis. This two-directional analysis is the only reliably defined and logically clear two-directional scheme of the five systems. Flanders works into the episode, which is a building up of units of analysis, but he reports no reliability for his episode unit. Additionally, it is suggested here that Flanders' major problem is his already large initial unit of analysis. Smith works in two directions, but since he rearranges his units of analysis, it is suggested here that they are not easily understandable or usable. Smith identifies a venture, identifies moves within a venture, and identifies strategies as either containing one move or a combination of moves. This leaves the relationship of ventures to strategies in a rather hazy area.

Of course, in enumerating the advantages of the Bellack system, one must be cognizant of the fact that the system was developed and used in a very structured classroom setting. When Bellack identifies two classroom tasks, one being substantive and the other instructional-logical, one might consider if this category definition would be appropriate to the coding of kindergarten free play activities or classes in the various arts.

Just because the question was raised as to whether the beginnings of a general classification system were possible, there is no reason to suppose that the field of curriculum and teaching needs *one* system of analysis to identify all aspects of classroom life. Indeed, it is this kind of question that this study hopes to ventilate. Perhaps a system of recording behavior on tape or film and then proceeding to analyze these tapes into several different category systems will be found to be just as useful, if not as efficient, a device as the use of *one* general classificatory system. The technique of multianalysis may be more appropriate in so complex an enterprise where many different kinds of information may be desired.

XV

Conclusion

In 1933 Dewey wrote:

> First, teachers have a habit of monopolizing continued discourse. Many if not most instructors would be surprised if informed at the end of the day of the amount of time they have talked as compared with any pupil. Children's conversation is often confined to answering questions in brief phrases or in single disconnected sentences. Expatiation and explanation are reserved for the teacher, who often admits any hint at an answer on the part of the pupil, and then amplifies what he supposes the child must have meant. The habits of sporadic and fragmentary discourse thus promoted have inevitably a disintegrating intellectual influence.[1]

Thirty years later the research findings on classroom behavior, with almost astounding unanimity, confirm Dewey's speculative assertions on the nature of the teacher-pupil verbal interaction.

Throughout the course of this book, where appropriate, areas that are still to be explored by curriculum researchers and theorists have been suggested. Now, in the final chapter, some restatements and additional remarks on this subject and others may be appropriate.

The need to test and retest those category systems which, like Bellack's, Flanders', and Hughes', have high reliability to determine their effectiveness under varied class patterns and at different age and grade levels, is perhaps the most pressing present need. Since investigation capable of relating one variable to another, thus providing explanation and after that prediction, must rely on a reliable and stable classification system, research work will not become cumulative unless one or more reliable, categorical bases exist upon which research can accumulate. The Smith category system must be rendered more reliable if it is to be effectively used. The Taba category system would certainly be enhanced if it were more reliable, but it is possible that her system will never be usable for those researchers who do not accept all the assumptions on the nature of thinking with which her categories are entwined.

---

[1] John Dewey, *How We Think*, rev. ed. (Boston: D. C. Heath and Co., 1933), p. 245.

The problem of the interlarding of untested theory or value judgments returns us once again to the issue of research and evaluation. Again the suggestion is made that the category system that is most theoretically unencumbered, most value free, and the least reflective of a particular view of teaching will serve the researcher best. The role of the researcher should be to provide a collection of tools to be put at the disposal of the teacher to render the classroom situation more controllable, more successful, and more predictable.

The statement was made earlier that longitudinal studies that would trace specific teachers, children, and classes over time might help in the identification of developmental school life patterns. Studies like the Carin study that identify classroom life from the perceptions of the participants (in his case it was the children's) would deepen our insight of school life. Studies of the outcomes in terms of students' and teachers' perceptions of particular classes or schooling experience would enable us to speak with greater confidence on the "meaning" of certain kinds of schooling activities.

More specific areas of investigation have suggested themselves as this study progressed. When researchers speak of the relation of teacher talk to pupil talk, what is being indicated is the talk of all pupils combined. An important area of investigation is this "pupil talk." It is a safe assumption that some students talk and others do not. In a sense some students are performers and others spectators in the classroom. Are the active participants different in their attitudes toward school, learning abilities, behavioral patterns? Taba tried to determine some of these relationships in her analysis of the high participator as a child who also produces "higher thought levels." It might be of interest to learn if the role of spectator or participant is stable from class to class for students.

Another area of investigation that these studies suggest but do not explore centers on the nature of the intensely oral-aural dimension of classroom life. Although we have readability formulas that can be used as rough estimates of the ease or difficulty of written language, there exists almost no information on the relative ease or difficulty of oral-aural communication. Although the researcher reports that one can categorize the classroom as a place where verbal behavior is almost constant, nothing is known of the amount, percentage, and degree of pupil understanding that accompanies their listening to "teacher talk." Indeed, this area is so undeveloped that there is no common vocabulary with which one can discuss such issues as listening as opposed to "critical listening," the relative merits for certain students of aural versus written communication, and why some persons understand aural instructions while others understand written instructions.

In the classrooms studied, as in most others throughout the nation if not the world, certain unexamined assumptions are inherent. The teacher speaks and assumes she is saying what she thinks she is saying. The students, when quiet, are assumed by the teacher to be listening. If the students are listening, the assumption is that they understand what the teacher thinks she is saying. At any point along this long chain of assumptions it may be possible to set up research studies that will find out for how many teachers and pupils any or all of these assumptions can be supported.

The problems of deriving the essence of the total speech act from a tapescript, which is then further translated by typing into written symbols, has already been discussed. The advantages of the taped observations, the ability to code after observations, the ability to code from a different perspective, and the ability to use different systems of analysis have also been discussed. One other set of advantages to be gained from tapescripts has not as yet been explored; this might be the use of mechanical tests on tapes to analyze voices in terms of dynamic range and stability of modulation. The brush sound reader makes a permanent record of voice dynamics. It would also be possible to identify voice range as well as count words per second and thus have some measure of rate of classroom speech. One might then be able to determine some of the qualities that are judged pleasant by pupils in teachers' speech. One might also eventually derive an idea of a proper rate of speech appropriate for different ages, grades, subjects, for maximum comprehension. The functions of repetition and emphasis might also be explored as investigations into speech and aural comprehension are pursued.

Although these studies are unique in many ways and comments that could appropriately be made of one could not similarly apply to the other four, one observation can be safely made of all five research studies. Each researcher while, on the one hand, offering the reader assurances of the tentative nature of his findings and the exploratory nature of his study, at some point will, with equal firmness, assure the reader that his particular study has identified *the* critically important aspect of classroom behavior, and will often make observations and offer suggestions for teacher training and classroom practice for which no evidence has been presented and which are entirely independent of the design of his study. Thus Flanders and Hughes urge teachers to reduce the *power* component in their teaching in order to promote student learning. Taba suggests that when teachers learn her system of teaching *thinking*, students will become better critical thinkers, more able to make inferences, generalizations, and predictions. Smith suggests that when teachers use the canons of logic with greater precision the students' initiative and creativity will be freed. Bellack, while not making suggestions for teachers' classroom behavior, does suggest what constitutes success for the teachers and pupils in terms of the *game* he hypothesizes. The fault pointed out here may be seen as one of "premature closure." The individual researcher whose work has been examined here seems too ready to see the total classroom picture through one aspect and to make judgments too quickly in terms of the one aspect he has investigated. As one reads the research report, one observes that speculations, inferences, and untested thoughts are often stated more positively than they should be. The research reports might better maintain an openness to different points of view, interpretation, and inference.

While in other fields it is not uncommon for the researcher to have his say at the conclusion of his study, independent of his evidence, the curriculum researcher must ask himself if he can be allowed this luxury. It is hardly a secret that teachers are not trained to read research reports. This being the case, there is a greater responsibility on the part of the researcher who deals with subjects of interest to the teacher to present his study and his findings with great clarity and, more important, with great restraint. The fields that permit the researcher a generous amount of extrapolation in his final chapter can hopefully depend on the ability of the research reader to be sensibly critical. Those who prepare research reports for the field of teaching should exercise great control in discussing their findings and clearly distinguish research findings from post-research speculation.

Research findings are often misused as a vehicle to force the support of one value position rather than another. It is important therefore to reaffirm here what was said differently earlier, that research findings do not indicate the "good," the "true," or the "beautiful." Research findings can demonstrate relationships; how these relationships are valued must be determined in contexts other than the research enterprise.

Bibliography

BOOKS

Arendt, Hannah. *Between Past and Future*. New York: Viking Press, 1961.

Baldwin, Alfred. *Behavior and Development in Childhood*. New York: Dryden Press, 1955.

Bartlett, F. D. *Thinking: An Experimental and Social Study*. New York: Basic Books, 1958.

Bellack, Arno A., Herbert M. Kliebard, Ronald T. Hyman, and Frank L. Smith. *The Language of the Classroom*. New York: Teachers College Press, 1966.

Bettelheim, Bruno. *Love Is Not Enough*. Glencoe, Ill.: The Free Press, 1950.

Brown, Roger. *Words and Things*. Glencoe, Ill.: The Free Press, 1958.

Bruner, Jerome S., Jacqueline J. Goodnow, and George A. Austin. *A Study of Thinking*. New York: John Wiley and Sons, 1956.

Conant, J. B. *The Education of American Teachers*. New York: McGraw-Hill Book Company, 1963.

Copi, Irving M. *Introduction to Logic*. Second ed. New York: Macmillan Company, 1961.

Dewey, John. *The Sources of a Science of Education*. New York: Horace Liveright, 1929.

Dewey, John. *How We Think*. Revised ed. Boston: D. C. Heath, 1933.

Dewey, John. *Democracy in Education*. New York: Macmillan Company, 1961.

Flavell, J. H. *The Developmental Psychology of Jean Piaget*. Princeton, N.J.: Van Nostrand, 1963.

Gross, Neal, Ward S. Mason, and Alexander W. McEachern. *Explorations in Role Analysis*. New York: John Wiley and Sons, 1958.

Hays, William L. *Statistics for Psychologists*. New York: Holt, Rinehart, and Winston, 1953.

Herbert, John, and John Swayze, *Wireless Observation*. New York: Horace Mann-Lincoln Institute of School Experimentation.

Kuhn, T. *The Structure of Scientific Revolutions*. Chicago: University of Chicago Press, 1962.

Murphy, Lois Barclay. *Personality in Young Children*. Vol. II. New York: Basic Books, Inc., 1957.

Peel, E. A. *The Pupil's Thinking*. London: Oldbourne, 1960.

Phenix, Phillip H. *Realms of Meaning: A Philosophy of the Curriculum for General Education*. New York: McGraw-Hill Book Company, 1964.

Prescott, Daniel. *The Child in the Educative Process*. New York: McGraw-Hill Book Company, 1957.

Scheffler, Israel. *The Language of Education*. Springfield, Mass.: Charles C Thomas, 1960.

Selltiz, Claire, Marie Jahoda, Morton Deutsch, and Stuart W. Cook. *Research Methods in Social Relations*. New York: Holt, Rinehart, and Winston, 1963.

Sherif, M., and C. W. Sherif. *Groups in Harmony and Tension*. New York: Harper and Brothers, 1953.

Simon, Anita, and E. Gill Boyer. *Mirrors for Behavior*, Philadelphia: Temple University, 1968.

Smith, B. Othanel, William O. Stanley, and J. Harlan Shores. *Fundamentals of Curriculum Development*. Revised ed. Yonkers-on-Hudson, New York: World Book Company, 1957.

Smith, B. Othanel, and Robert H. Ennis (eds.). *Language and Concepts in Education*. Chicago: Rand McNally and Company, 1961.

Stratemeyer, Florence B., Hamden L. Forkner, Margaret G. McKim, and A. Harry Passow (eds.) *Developing a Curriculum for Modern Living*. Second ed. New York: Teachers College, Columbia University, 1957.

Taba, Hilda. *Curriculum Development, Theory and Practice*. New York: Harcourt, Brace, and World, 1962.

Walker, Helen M., and Joseph Lev. *Statistical Inference*. New York: Holt, Rinehart, and Winston, 1953.

Waller, Willard. *The Sociology of Teaching*. New York: John Wiley and Sons, 1932.

Wellman, Carl. *The Language of Ethics*. Cambridge, Mass.: Harvard University Press, 1961.

Wertheimer, M. *Productive Thinking*. New York: Harper and Brothers, 1945.

Wheelis, Allen. *Quest for Identity*. New York: W. W. Norton and Company, 1958.

Wilson, John. *Language and the Pursuit of Truth*. Cambridge, England: University Press, 1958.

Wittgenstein, Ludwig. *Philosophical Investigations*. Oxford, England: Basil Blackwell, 1958.

PUBLICATIONS OF THE GOVERNMENT, LEARNED SOCIETIES, AND OTHER ORGANIZATIONS

Bellack, Arno.A. (ed.). *Theory and Research in Teaching*. New York: Bureau of Publications, Teachers College, Columbia University, 1963.

Calderwood, James D. *International Economic Problems*. Minneapolis, Minn.: Curriculum Resources, Inc., 1961.

Dewey, John. *Theory of Valuation*. Chicago: University of Chicago Press, 1939.

Flanders, Ned A. *Teacher Influence, Pupil Attitudes, and Achievement*. Cooperative Research Monograph No. 12. Washington, D.C.: U.S. Department of Health, Education, and Welfare. Office of Education, 1965.

Joint Committee of Technical Recommendations for Psychological Tests and Diagnostic Techniques. Washington, D. C.: American Psychological Association, Inc., 1954.

Mitzel, Harold E., and W. Rabinowitz. *Assessing Social-Emotional Climate in the Classroom by Withall's Technique*. Psychological Monographs, No. 368, 1953.

Passow, A. Harry (ed.). *Curriculum Crossroads*. New York: Bureau of Publications, Teachers College, Columbia University, 1962.

PERIODICALS

Anderson, H. H. "The Measurement of Domination and of Socially Integrated Behavior in Teachers' Contacts with Children," *Child Development*, 10:73–89, June, 1939.

Aschner, Mary Jane. "Language of Teaching," *Teachers College Record*, 61:242–252, February, 1960.

Bernstein, Basil. "Social Structure, Language, and Learning," *Educational Research*, 3:163–167, June, 1961.

Cogan, M. L. "Theory and Design of a Study of Teacher-Pupil Interaction," *The Harvard Educational Review*, 26:315–342, Fall, 1956.

Flanders, Ned A., J. P. Anderson, and E. J. Amidon. "Measuring Dependence Proneness in the Classroom," *Educational and Psychological Measurement*, 21:575–587, Autumn, 1961.

Hoyt, C. J. and C. L. Stunkard. "Estimation of Test Reliability for Unrestricted Item Scoring Methods," *Educational and Psychological Measurements*, 12:756–758, May, 1952.

Hughes, Marie, and Associates. "Teaching Is Interaction," *Elementary School Journal*, 58:457–464, May, 1958.

Jackson, Phillip. "The Way Teaching Is," *National Education Association Journal*, 54:10–13, November, 1965.

Jersild, Arthur T., and Margaret F. Meigs. "Direct Observation as a Research Method," *Review of Educational Research*, 9:472–482, December, 1939.

Kagan, J., H. A. Moss, and I. E. Sigel. "Conceptual Style and the Use of Affect Labels," *Merrill-Palmer Quarterly of Behavior and Development*, 6:261–278, July, 1960.

Lippitt, Ronald, and R. L. White. "Patterns of Aggressive Behavior in Experimentally Created 'Social Climates,'" *Journal of Social Psychology*, 10:271–299, May, 1939.

McMurray, Foster. "Preface to an Autonomous Discipline of Education," *Educational Theory*, 5:129–140, July, 1955.

Olson, W. D., and B. O. Hughes. "Concepts of Growth—Their Significance to Teachers," *Childhood Education*, 21:53–63, October, 1944.

Page, E. B. "Behavioral Theory, Verbal Magic and Education," *Educational Theory*, 12:73–78, April, 1962.

Perkins, H. V. "Climate Influences Group Learning," *Journal of Educational Research*, 45:115–119, October, 1951.

Smith, B. O. "A Concept of Teaching," *Teachers College Record* 5:229–241, February, 1960.

Taba, Hilda. "The Problems in Developing Critical Thinking," *Progressive Education*, 28:45–48, November, 1950.

Thorndike, Robert L. "Two Screening Tests of Verbal Intelligence of the American Adult," *The Journal of Applied Psychology*, 26:128–135, April, 1942.

Thorndike, Robert L., and George H. Gallup. "Verbal Intelligence of the American Adult," *The Journal of General Psychology*, 30:75–85, January, 1944.

Trow, W. C., A. E. Zander, W. C. Morse, and D. H. Jenkins. "Psychology of Group Behavior: The Class as a Group," *Journal of Educational Psychology*, 41:322–338, October, 1950.

Tyler, Ralph. "Conditions for Effective Learning," *National Education Association Journal*, 48:47–49, September, 1959.

Vinacke, W. E. "Stereotyping among National Racial Groups in Hawaii: A Study in Ethnocentrism," *Journal of Social Psychology*, 11:265-270, August, 1949.

Withall, John. "Assessment of the Social-Emotional Climates Experienced by a Group of Seventh Graders as They Move from Class to Class," *Educational and Psychological Measurement*, 12:440–451, Autumn, 1952.

UNPUBLISHED MATERIALS

Amidon, E. J. "Dependent-Prone Students in Experimental Learning Situations," Unpublished Ph.D. Thesis, University of Minnesota, Minneapolis, 1959.

Aschner, Mary Jane. "The Analysis of Classroom Discourse: A Method and Its Uses." Unpublished Ph.D. Thesis, University of Illinois, Urbana, 1959.

Bellack, Arno A., and Joel B. Davitz. "The Language of the Classroom." U.S. Department of Health, Education, and Welfare, Cooperative Research Program, Project No. 1497. New York: Institute of Psychological Research, Teachers College, Columbia University, 1963.

Bellack, Arno A. "The Language of the Classroom." U.S. Department of Health, Education, and Welfare, Cooperative Research Program, Project No. 2023. New York: Institute of Psychological Research, Teachers College, Columbia University, 1965.

Carin, Arthur. "Children's Perception of Selected Teaching Acts." Unpublished Doctoral Project Report, University of Utah, Salt Lake City, 1959.

Flanders, Ned A. "Teacher Influence, Pupil Attitudes, and Achievement." U.S. Office of Education Cooperative Research Project No. 397. Minneapolis: University of Minnesota, 1960.

Galloway, Charles M. "An Exploratory Study of Observational Procedures for Determining Teacher Non-verbal Communication." Unpublished Doctoral Project Report, University of Florida, Gainesville, 1962.

Hughes, Marie M., and Associates. "The Assessment of the Quality of Teaching: A Research Report." U.S. Office of Education Cooperative Research Project No. 353. Salt Lake City: University of Utah, 1959.

Kliebard, Herbert M. "Teaching Cycles: A Study of the Pattern and Flow of the Classroom Discourse." Unpublished Doctoral Project Report, Teachers College, Columbia University, New York, 1963.

Smith, B. Othanel, and Milton O. Meux, in collaboration with others. "A Study of the Logic of Teaching." Urbana: Bureau of Educational Research, College of Education, 1963.

Smith, B. Othanel, and Milton O. Meux. "A Tentative Report on Strategies of Teaching." U.S. Office of Education Department of Health, Education, and Welfare, Project No. 1640. Urbana: Bureau of Educational Research, College of Education, University of Illinois, 1964.

Taba, Hilda, and others. "Thinking in Elementary School Children." U.S. Department of Health, Education, and Welfare, Cooperative Research Program, Project No. 1574. San Francisco: San Francisco State College, 1964.

ARTICLES IN COLLECTIONS

Getzels, J., and P. Jackson. "The Teacher Personality and Characteristics." American Educational Research Association *Handbook of Research on Teaching*. N. L. Gage, editor. Chicago: Rand McNally, 1963.

Jenkins, David H., and Ronald Lippitt. "Interpersonal Perceptions in the Classroom." *Adolescent: A Book of Readings*. Jerome Seidman, editor. New York: Dryden Press, 1953.

Langer, Susanne K. "The Growing Center." *Frontiers of Knowledge*. Lynn White, Jr., editor. New York: Harper and Brothers, 1956.

Medley, Donald, and Harold E. Mitzel. "Measuring Classroom Behavior by Systematic Observation." American Educational Research Association *Handbook of Research on Teaching*. N. L. Gage, editor. Chicago: Rand McNally, 1963.

DICTIONARIES

Thorndike-Barnhart. *Comprehensive Desk Dictionary*. Clarence L. Barnhart, editor. Garden City, N.Y.: Doubleday and Company, 1951.

Webster's New Collegiate Dictionary. Springfield, Mass.: G. and C. Merriam Company, 1961.

Index

Anderson, H. H., 17
Arendt, Hannah, 32
Aschner, Mary Jane, 55, 56, 62
"Assessment of the Quality of Teaching," 2
  description, 8, 9
  design and scope, 77, 78
  outline, 108-113
Assumptions, 53-72
  Bellack, 53, 54, 56, 60-63
  Flanders, 53, 55, 56, 58, 63-67
  Hughes, 53, 54, 58, 63-67
  Smith, 54, 56, 58, 67
  Taba, 54, 59, 67-72

Baldwin, Alfred, 13
Bellack, Arno, 1, 2, 128, 132
  assumptions, 53, 54, 56, 60-63
  category systems
    discussion, 16, 17, 19, 144-147, 150
    outline, 91-101
  design and scope of study, 73-74, 79
  effectiveness of study, 134-136
  findings, 47, 48
  observation systems, 83, 86, 87
  observer effect, 80, 81
  outline of study, 6, 7
  sample, 45
  statistical systems, 97, 99
  valuing, 33
  verbal behavior, 52
Bettleheim, Bruno, 49
Boyer, E. Gill, 90
Brown, Roger, 68
Bruner, Jerome, 68

Calderwood, James, 6, 73
Carin, Arthur, 46, 47, 53, 54, 148
Categories of definition, 25
Category systems, 15-19, 22, 142-150
  discussion
    Bellack, 16, 17, 19, 144-147, 150
    Flanders, 17-19, 142-147, 149
    Hughes, 17-19, 144, 145, 147, 149

Category systems (*continued*)
    Smith, 16, 17, 19, 144, 145, 149
    Taba, 18, 19, 147-149
  outline, 91-127
    Bellack, 91-101
    Flanders, 101-108
    Hughes, 108-113
    Smith, 113-120
    Taba, 121-127
  valuing discussion 29-38
"Children's Perceptions of Selected Teaching Acts"; 46, 47 *see also* Carin, Arthur
Classroom
  behavior, 2
  climate, 7, 17
  description, 22
  interaction, 1
  logic, 36
  observation, 22, 40, 41
Classroom language game, 7
  conveyed meanings, 60, 61, 62
Cogan, M. L., 17, 56
Cognitive
  learning, 18
  processes, 11
Communication
  enhancing, 36
  problems of in research, 25-28
Conant, James, 19, 21, 64
Content analysis, 60, 142
Cook, Stuart W., 15
Curriculum,
  definition, 25
  Taba experimental, 11
Curriculum and teaching, 1, 3
  definitions, 25, 26
  descriptive and prescriptive theory, 19-22
Definitions
  discussion, 25
  stipulative, 28
Design and scope of studies
  Bellack, 73, 74, 79
  Flanders, 74-79
  Hughes, 77-79
  Smith, 78, 79
  Taba, 78, 79